Connect
To The Light

Rediscover Truth

Though the information within the pages is researched and documented, it is a reference book for educational purpose only. The information is *not* intended to prescribe treatment or *cure* conditions. The reader shall be made aware that this information is *not* intended as medical advice and *not* intended to be used in place of medical treatment. It is merely the sharing of knowledge and information from the research and experience of the author. The reader is strongly encouraged to do further research. If medical *problems* are prevalent and persist, please consult your doctor. You are highly encouraged to make your own health care decisions, based upon your own research, along with your health care professional. You are totally responsible for your own self if you choose to do anything based on what you have learned within these pages.

Connect To The Light
Receive Joy

Receive Joy Publishing
Naples, Florida, U.S.A.

© 2019 Receive Joy
Carisa Jones, Sylvia Lehmann
All rights reserved.
Cover photography by Steven C. Jones © 2017

ISBN: 978-0-9988484-1-9

Receive Joy, LLC
www.receivejoy.com
ask@receivejoy.com

DEDICATION

This book is dedicated to the Trinity:
God, Jesus, and The Holy Spirit.

CONTENTS

Introduction 1

Part One—Connect!

1. Connect To The Light 7
2. Connect First 25
3. The Grand Doors Of My Life 42
4. Collecting Data On Myself 56
5. My Divine Mission 87
6. Feel The Connection 98

Part Two—Stay Connected!

7. Prayer 115
8. Contemplative Meditation 133
9. Read The Holy Bible 142
10. Community 150
11. Flow With Nature 158
12. Receive Joy 165
13. Contribution 172

14.	Journaling	183
15.	Live By Design	191
16.	Be The Light	227

Connect—Pocketguide	237
Acknowledgments	253
Million True Millionaires	255
Available From Receive Joy	257

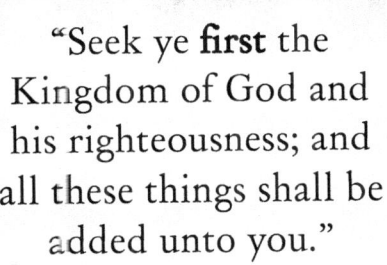

"Seek ye **first** the Kingdom of God and his righteousness; and all these things shall be added unto you."

—Matthew 6:33 (KJV)

INTRODUCTION

When we place a cake mix in the oven, after we have combined together all the ingredients listed on the back, if the oven is still off, or if we turn it on after our mix has been in the oven for 30 minutes, the outcome is different than if we had precisely followed the baking instructions. The instructions generally recommend to turn the oven on **first**. It says "Step One: Preheat oven." To heat, the oven has to be plugged in and turned on for the cake mix to bake correctly into a cake. It is paramount to do Step One first. First connect: Plug in and turn on.

Welcome to Step One of Receive Joy's *Ask And You Shall Receive* Nine Step Method to Consciously Create. This book dives deeper into Step One: Connect. It contains many additional insights about **why** it is important to connect first, **ways** to connect, and ways to **stay connected** to the Light of God.

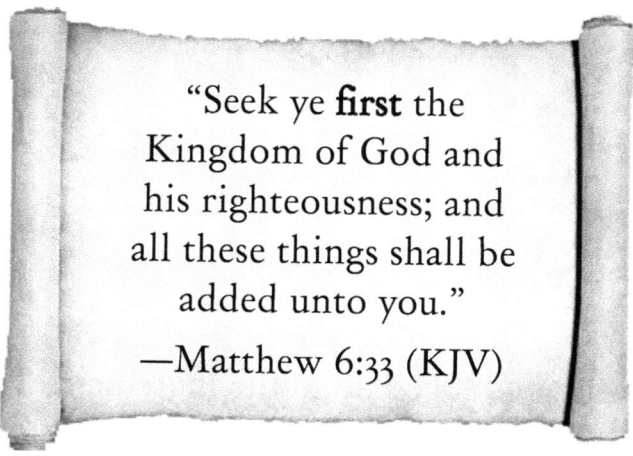

"Seek ye **first** the Kingdom of God and his righteousness; and all these things shall be added unto you."
—Matthew 6:33 (KJV)

Receive Joy has written *Connect To The Light* to guide and encourage a permanent and more personal connection with God and to help everyone take responsibility to live their life by conscious design. This is the point where we have to make a conscious decision: Are we of this world or of God's world? Are we aligning our will to God's will, surrendering completely, and living by intricate design? Let us understand that God is the Power of the Universe and we gain life in and through Him. "*Luck*" and "*co-incidence*" are fabrications of this world. Absolute power and divine order are the very fabric of God's supernatural plan. This book will help us to connect to this ultimate, mighty power source. God is the light.

Introduction

"Part One: Connect!" explains in detail what it means to be connected to the light, why it is important to connect first, and what we can learn about ourself to spark the desire to live by design. By the end of Part One, everyone shall have discovered their current divine mission and trust in their all-knowing.

"Part Two: Stay Connected!" offers enlightening examples to establish a connection and stay connected to God, day by day, moment by moment.

Let us ask ourself to open our heart and consciousness to have God's light shine in and through us. Let us reach out into these new areas of understanding and welcome them in. Let us open our heart and our mind now and journey to a new and more powerful, focused and loved, light and easy, aware and **connected** YOU! Let us connect and live by design!

Connect To The Light

Before we begin, let us take several deep breaths very slowly.

As you breathe in say to yourself

"Here I am God. I am connected to You."

As you breathe out say

"My mind is wide open. I allow myself to receive."

And so we are present and ready.

Part One

Chapter 1

CONNECT TO THE LIGHT

Look up. Look up at the sky. We see the blue. It is vast. There is so much more out there than what is underneath our feet and immediately around us. There is more in the atmosphere than the air we breathe. There is an in-visible force that surrounds all. There is a Power. The Universe is full of Power.

We all agree that there is something powerful, tremendous, awesome, and mysterious out there which is greater than ourself and part of ourself. It is outside of us and it is inside of us. And although we may sometimes feel we are separate from it, **we are indeed connected** to it. As it surrounds us, it literally fills every cell and the space between them. It fills all matter.

Connect To The Light

We all come from this Power and are part of it. It is greater than our individual self. It provides continual abundance. It is formulated from love. It contains all **light and life**. It is magnificent, it is free, and it is equally available to all of us. It supports and embraces all life. Somehow, we have an inner knowledge that we are from this vast Heavenly Power containing continual awesome perfection.

This power is a beautiful energy that exists and is full of absolute intelligence. It is consistent and flows progressively. Let us first connect to this Divine Power so that we can access and call on it.

This Power is called by many names. We call this Divine Power Source God, because it is so wonderful to know this source of light as a loving parental persona. Thus, we are more drawn to develop and maintain an intimate relationship with Him.

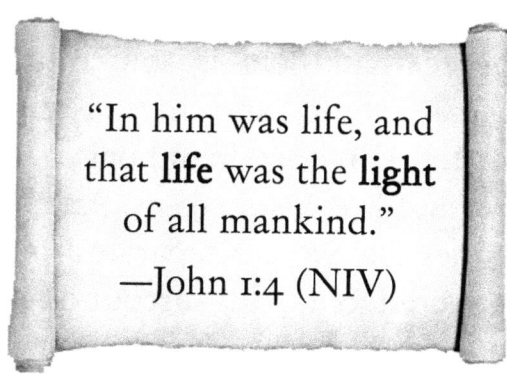

"In him was life, and that **life** was the **light** of all mankind."
—John 1:4 (NIV)

Connect To The Light

Connection is essential for humankind. We often depend on worldly sources: ourself, others, nature. However, God is the one true source to be connected to. He is life. He is light. Plug into this powerful relationship offered to you. God wishes for us to activate our connection to Him. It is God's first commandment:

> "Jesus replied: 'Love the Lord your God with all your heart and with all your soul and with all your mind.' This is the **first** and greatest commandment."
> —Matthew 22:37-38 (NIV)

God offers us this life-changing connection. He is in and around us. Let us be aware of this existing, available connection.

We are eternal beings with physical bodies, living within a Quantum World. As we are vibrational beings, we oscillate at the same vibration with God. We all live vibrationally connected by our matching frequencies to His abundant Source of Energy. Filled with this light energy, we are always vibrating with it.

This abundant Source Light Energy contains a constant understanding and honoring of all life forms. It is **reactive to us**. Our thoughts, focus, feelings, and words continually summon this energy. It is all-loving and all-providing, full of continual possibilities.

When we are aligned with the perfect vibration of love and light, we are connected with God's Light. In this Light, all is well. When we choose to match our vibrational power to the Almighty Power, we regain our birthright. Our birthright is to be consciously connected and powered by God's Power Source, allowing us to flow light and easy throughout our life.

In our physical realm, the realm we experience with our senses, light is a type of energy; an electromagnetic radiation of any wavelength. Less than one percent of the electromagnetic spectrum is visible to the human eye. Amazingly, this range of visible light allows us to see all the world's beauty in color. Light has the nature of both wave and particle, which is referred to as wave-particle duality. Each wave can be measured with a wavelength and a frequency. Light particles exist everywhere in small energy packets called photons. A photon is an energy particle that moves at high speed. We are made of photons and photon light is in every cell of our body. Photons make up about 99 percent of our body's atoms and cells, and signal all body parts to carry out their functions. Light is always here, in us and around us, and readily available.

> "Then God said
> 'Let there be **light**';
> and there was **light**."
> —Genesis 1:3 (NIV)

With the first words God spoke in the Bible, He spoke light into existence, and so it is. He chose to create light first. As God is very accurate, the light was of immense importance. He created an abundance of light.

> "The Lord wraps himself
> in **light** as with a garment;
> he stretches out the
> heavens like a tent"
> —Psalm 104:2 (NIV)

Connect To The Light

In our spiritual realm, the realm of faith, God is the source of light. The light of God is in every particle in and around us. The divine particles of God's Holy Spirit are in every cell of our body. Let us recognize this divine part of us. The light in us is already connected to the light of God.

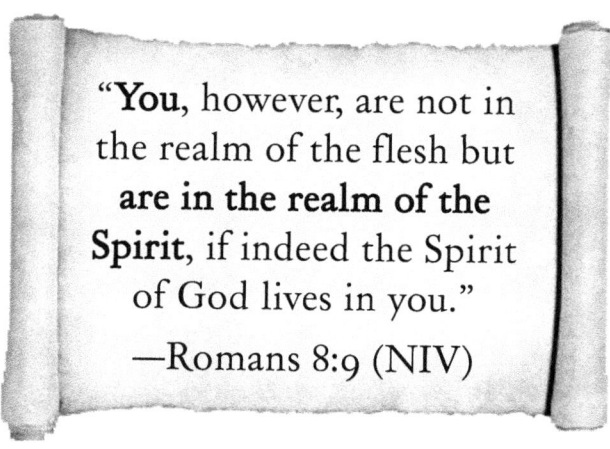

"**You**, however, are not in the realm of the flesh but **are in the realm of the Spirit**, if indeed the Spirit of God lives in you."
—Romans 8:9 (NIV)

The light is the Almighty Power and His glory. It is God's presence. The light is God's love. It shows us the wonder of His being. The light is the eternal force of God's divine love inside each of us. God is presently stirring in every atom inside of us and around us. He is also the space between all particles. He is the space that connects all of us. This space is beyond the perception of most of our senses. He is always present, always with us, He surrounds us; above, below, inside, and outside. God is omnipresent. He is present everywhere at the same time and inhabits the whole Universe. God is omnipotent. His power is the greatest. God is omniscient. His all-knowing encompasses the past, present, and future. God is always with us in **supernatural ways**.

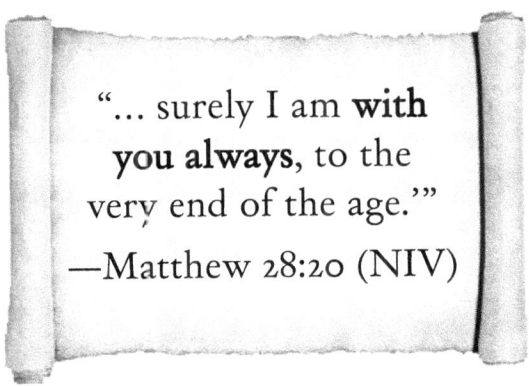

"… surely I am **with you always**, to the very end of the age.'"
—Matthew 28:20 (NIV)

We are in continual connection through His light.

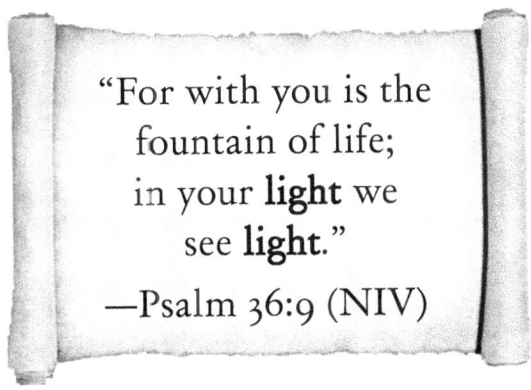

"For with you is the fountain of life;
in your **light** we see **light**."
—Psalm 36:9 (NIV)

Connect To The Light

He created our mind and our body in a way that we function like electrical devices. We have the ability to connect – to plug in and stay turned on; or to live in the illusion of *"separation"* from the power source and *"turned off"* and *"unplugged."* It is our decision. Our true potential can only be reached when we are plugged in and turned on. To actively take part in our life and use our co-creation power in good ways, this important connection shall be established. When we decide to use this light energy, God's love and light have the strength to light our life, sustain us, and bring us prosperity.

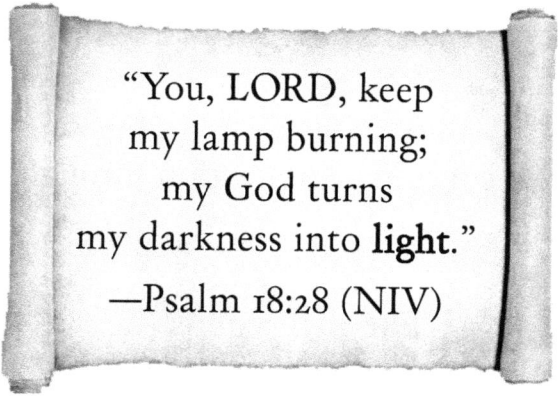

"You, LORD, keep
my lamp burning;
my God turns
my darkness into **light**."
—Psalm 18:28 (NIV)

God lives inside of us, moves inside of us, and is with us all the time. Be encouraged to further develop a personal relationship with God. Once we recognize Him with our heart, ask Him to guide us all day long.

Connect To The Light

Let us keep our channel of communication open to Him. Let us call on Him with our thoughts, words, and deeds. Once we are consciously connected and the channel is open, we are plugged in and ready to live by design.

> "'For I know the plans I have for you,' declares the LORD, 'plans to **prosper** you and not to harm you, plans to give you **hope** and **a future**.'"
>
> —Jeremiah 29:11 (NIV)

We are promised that when our hearts are connected to Him we will **prosper**. Our connection to God gives us **hope**, which is an expectation for a great, positive outcome, and **a future**.

Connect To The Light

Let us look at other reasons why we desire an intimate relationship with our Creator:

1. He **Created** us: At some point or another, we all ask ourself the existential questions: Who am I? Why am I here? Being connected to God answers these questions. We are here with a purpose. We are here because He created us in His image. He counted every hair on our head and He has a mighty plan for each of us. We know that there is something awesome watching over us. God supports and comforts us.

2. He gives us **Wisdom** and **All-knowing**: He left us with His Holy Spirit. The Holy Spirit knows all things, certainly He knows our plans. We can draw on God's profound joyful wisdom any time and in any circumstance. God instructs and leads us. We know what we shall move toward and what to stay away from.

3. He gives us **Alignment**: The more aware we are of our connection, the more our will aligns with God's will. Let us align our head with our heart.

4. We are **Attracted** to Him: We are drawn to the source of perfection and purity. We are drawn to and resonate with the source from which we come.

5. He is **Love**: All love just exists. We can draw on God's love to fill us and pass through us to light all humanity. Love is a desired feeling. God loves us first, and the beautiful feeling of His divine love for us is one of the biggest reasons we desire to be connected. Connecting to the light begins by believing that we are worthy of God's love. We are worthy because we are His children and He loves us just as we are.

6. He instilled **Gratitude** within us: We view our world friendly when we have a mindset of gratitude. There is so much to be grateful for in every moment. Let us be thankful and give thanks.

7. He left us **Gifts**: Jesus and the Holy Spirit are our greatest gift. He also gave each of us individual gifts. When we are connected, we are aware of our gifts and talents and use them throughout our life to bring joy to His kingdom.

8. We have **Confidence** in Him: To know we are supported, loved, always connected, and purpose-filled, leads to increased faith and confidence. We have plenty of role models in the Bible who went forth in absolute confidence. Just think of Jesus, Abraham, Moses, Esther, Daniel, David, and Noah.

9. He shares **Community** with us: We are communing with our Creator. He is with us always. We are each a part of His great plan. We came into this world alone with our Creator and we will leave this world alone with our Creator. Let us practice being alone with our Creator.

10. He supplies **Salvation** and **Life Everlasting**: Jesus died on the cross so that we who believe in Him have eternal life. He delivered us, now we can rejoice and live forevermore.

11. He provides **Fulfillment**: We all know people who seemingly "have it all" yet are still searching for happiness. Having a true connection to God's light fills our life with meaning and rightmindedness, happiness, and joy. Let us make the most of, and be pleased and fulfilled with, our life!

> 12. He brings **Renewal**: When we are connected, we tap into the illuminating renewal force of God's power. He forgives and makes us new every day.
>
> 13. He allows us to be in **Co-Creation** with Him: God loves us so much that He allows us to be co-creators with Him. Ask, seek, knock with thanksgiving, prayer, petition, and supplication.
>
> 14. God is **Peace**: When we are connected to the light, we can rest and relax in God's everlasting almighty arms. His light guides us in the way of powerful peace.

We have a lot to gain from our connection to the light. We may have additional reasons why we wish to be connected to God. This is a growing list of praise for Him. Please feel free to contact me at ask@receivejoy.com to add to the list.

One day I was on the way to the airport. Using the time, I was saying to God, "Show me something wonderful today as I am in joy." I drove past a billboard that stated **"Wise men still seek Him."** This gave me an elevated feeling of joy in my heart and put a smile on my face. The next day, my daughter and I went to a thrift store. As I walked into the store my eyes went to a shelf where three small porcelain figures were displayed: The three wise kings from the nativity scene. I immediately bought them and put them on my own shelf to be reminded daily that wise men still seek Him: God, the Creator of all. As a bonus gift I received a beautiful leather-bound Bible with large print for $1 at the thrift store.

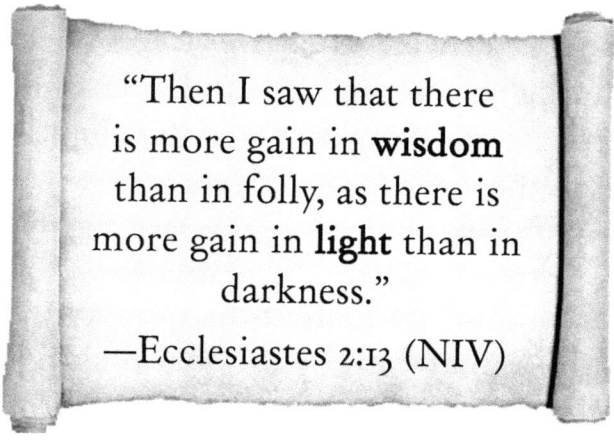

"Then I saw that there is more gain in **wisdom** than in folly, as there is more gain in **light** than in darkness."
—Ecclesiastes 2:13 (NIV)

Let us step out from under the shadow of "self" and into the light of the Lord. We are connecting to God's greatness and we are connecting to our own inner greatness that He created in each of us. It is as if we are harnessed onto a parasailing boat. We are connected with a big buckle in the center of our chest which is harnessed onto the parachute that is lifting us up to fly. God is that parachute lifting us up. And when we mindfully connect, we are securely harnessed onto Him. We give Him permission and we can lift our hands, arms, and legs as He is lifting us into our greatness. He is in charge. We have a much better life full of greatness when we stay lifted up. Let us stay connected and check that our harness is buckled to God.

Another great analogy is to visualize ourself as an astronaut floating in space. We are joyfully floating, knowing that we are hooked onto our space shuttle, God. We are hooked on and we have this secure rope or cord floating along with us. Because we are attached, we can float confidently, look around, and enjoy the wonder of humanity's existence.

We are tethered onto something awesome! Let us stay tethered onto that. Be aware of anything earthly that we may have temporarily tethered onto. If we are truly changing and growing, we are required to lay down our old stories, worn out beliefs, and illusions. Starting now.

Before we take any action, we shall ask ourself: Are we calm? Are we aligned? Are we connected? Are we yoked to Christ? Matthew 11:30 promises a light and easy life for the one walking with Jesus and the Holy Spirit.

Connect To The Light

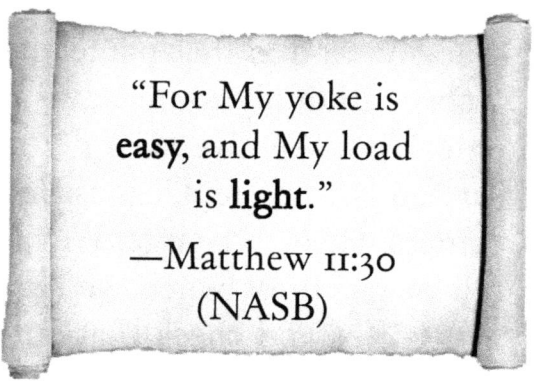

"For My yoke is **easy,** and My load is **light**."
—Matthew 11:30 (NASB)

When we are **connected to the Light**, our consciousness is spiritualized. We see the world through God's eyes and experience it with His heart. The connection gives us strength, confidence, and happiness. This connection is a harness. We are attached. We are yoked to Christ. We have a life vest on and a parachute strapped to us. We are attached to the "boat" below, yet soaring above in confidence and joy.

We function like magnetic frequency generators. We come equipped with two major energy centers to connect to the Power Source: Our head and our heart—our heart being the more powerful. Interestingly, research at the HeartMath Institute in Boulder Creek, California, revealed that the heart has an electric force 100 times stronger and a magnetic force 5,000 times stronger than the brain.

Our hearts create frequency vibrations through our feelings, just as our brain creates frequency vibrations through our thoughts. The heart is first to develop during gestation in the womb, and when fully grown contains about 40,000 neurons.

When our head and our heart are in alignment, our life is light and easy and we are yoked to Christ. All that is required of us is to mindfully connect and rise to our true potential. Please consider that it is time that we know something about humanity we have yet to think about and dream of: In us is more energy than we can ever imagine, we have more talent than we know exists, and more power and more creation waiting to be tapped into than we will ever use. We are filled with God's Holy Spirit! Let us be illuminated with His glory.

Annually around Christmas, a friend of mine collects donations to fill shoe boxes for a Shoebox Ministry with her church. The boxes are donated and shipped all over the world. One year when she was just finishing up the final of 5,000 boxes, she had a single sock left over and was wondering what to do with it. She decided to put it in the last box, thinking

Connect To The Light

it may possibly be used. Months later, she received a weathered letter in the mail from Vietnam. It said, "Thank you for the one sock for my one foot." God is so miraculous!

Chapter 2

CONNECT FIRST

In the process of truly deciding to make changes in our life and to begin living by design, let us start with the understanding that we function like an electrical device. Any device, such as a toaster or hairdryer, just sits there until we plug it in and turn it on. We sometimes attempt to turn on our gadgets before plugging them in. "Does this device work?" we ask. Once we check the connection, we realize simply plugging it in is the answer. When we use an electrical device, let us plug in the cord and connect it to an active power source. Only then is it useful.

We are like a wonderful device ourself and we can connect to and harness all power. In order to make the most of ourself during this earthly life, let us connect to the Power Source and turn on. We were designed and created to live connected, plugged in and powered on, in order to do great things, be positive, and be joyful. Let us function at our highest potential and accomplish what we were created for.

The strongest power source in this world is the Power of the Universe. God is the power. He is the Power of the Universe. He is the Light of the whole world. He is the gift and the giver. He designed this Universe as a perfect delivery system already stocked with a total abundance of love, happiness, health, wealth, wisdom, and more. Our first choice is to plug in, turn on, and thus connect to Him! Connect to God's grace: His perfect holiness.

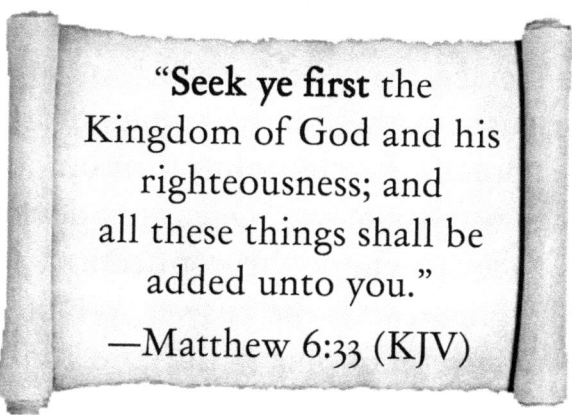

"**Seek ye first** the Kingdom of God and his righteousness; and all these things shall be added unto you."
—Matthew 6:33 (KJV)

Let us look at the word **first**. "First" to me is the moment our eyes open. The first thing we always check when our eyes open in the morning is our connection to God. Are we plugged into the Source Light Energy? Are we connected so we can use all this greatness?

Connect First

Some of us wait to start praying at the breakfast table or when we are on our way to work. However, the Bible verse states "**Seek ye first**." Our toaster and the hairdryer only turn on when they are plugged in first.

To help us feel our connection, we look up at the sky, we look up to our Heavenly Father, we look up in the air. We look up to what there is most of on this planet and it is all free. This is the most exciting part, it is all free. It is the open air. There is more air than anything else. There is more air out there than trees, grass, sand, and water. Think about it—what is there most of? As we look up to God's heavenly realm we see the open air. God is in this space. It is miraculous that out of the thin air comes everything.

When we connect to God, we become fully engaged in the present moment. With every breath we realize that we are present. This realization is amazing! Our breath of life is the basis for everything. Humans can exist free of food for days or even months; free of water for days; however, free of air, we can exist only minutes.

Let us plug in the minute we wake up, "Here I am, God!", and check that we are turned on. Let us be aware of our breath in the moment. Let us be mindful and take three deep breaths and focus only on our inhalation and our exhalation.

Let us do it right now!

Connect To The Light

Relax and soften your shoulders. Gently touch your tongue to the roof of your mouth. Breathe in and out through the nose. Take a full breath deep in your diaphragm. Push your belly out as you inhale. Push your bottom down into your chair. Imagine the oxygen reaching every cell in your body. Softly hold your breath a short moment. Flatten your belly as you gently exhale. Relax your shoulders even more.

Repeat this breathing pattern three times. Inhale deeply. Exhale fully. Inhale deeply. Exhale fully. Inhale deeply. Exhale fully.

As you breathe in, say to yourself, "Here I am God. I am connected to You."

As you breathe out, say, "My mind is wide open. I allow myself to receive."

Throughout the day repeat this breathing pattern as often as you wish.

Connect First

Let us practice this! Intentional deep breathing is a wonderful exercise to engage in all day long. Thus, we connect to our inner power source with our breath. Breathe with intent. All our cells require oxygen. Oxygen activates our self-healing. Next, let us connect to the outer great power source of God, the power of the Universe.

> Here I am, God.
> I am plugged in to You.
> I love You. Let's do this. You've got this. You've got me. Let's start anew. Let's begin now.

Throughout the day there are many firsts. Let us check our connection every time before we start anything: Opening our eyes, jumping out of bed, using the bathroom, eating, swimming, driving; **first is first!**

"**Seek ye first** the kingdom of God." Let us check and declare our connection, our presence, and start communicating with God. Also, when we wake up from vivid dreams and these dreams seem to follow us into the day, we shall first connect and then re-create these dreams, making them better with happier plots and endings.

Let us remember to check our connection throughout the day, asking God's blessing first, before we proceed with each activity. "Seek ye **first** the kingdom of God" and check the connection. Let us check the cord: Am I plugged in and turned on? Now it is time to plug back in and power on.

As we are paying attention to our breathing and declaring our presence, we may say a beautiful prayer. The following prayer is based on the Prayer of Jabez that can be found in 1 Chronicles 4:10 in the Holy Bible.

> *Dear God,*
> *bless me,*
> *expand my territory,*
> *wrap Your arms around me,*
> *and keep me in*
> *Your righteous arena.*

This is a great example of being plugged in. In this Old Testament passage, God inspired the scripture listing a long lineage of the descendants of Judah. Suddenly He interrupted the list to single out and honor Jabez. He brings our attention to the prayer Jabez cries out passionately to the Lord. It is amazing that in this prayer, Jabez is calling on God, "bless **me**, God" and he is **praying for himself first**. With his prayer Jabez is plugging in. All is between him and God.

The following examples illustrate why it is important for us to connect to God first: Prior to an airplane taking off, the flight attendant reminds us that in the event of an emergency, to first put on our air mask before we assist others. Why do the airlines remind us to help ourself first? Only through caring for ourself can we have the strength to assist others. Another example of this is drawing on our bank account. Money is first deposited in our account before good checks can be written. Also, we can only jump in after a swimmer to rescue them if we are a capable swimmer ourself. Our cup shall be full, before it runneth over. **Let us develop ourself first.**

Once we know that we are plugged in and connected, we can actually turn on. To make the most of our wonderful device throughout this earthly life, we connect to God and we receive His righteousness.

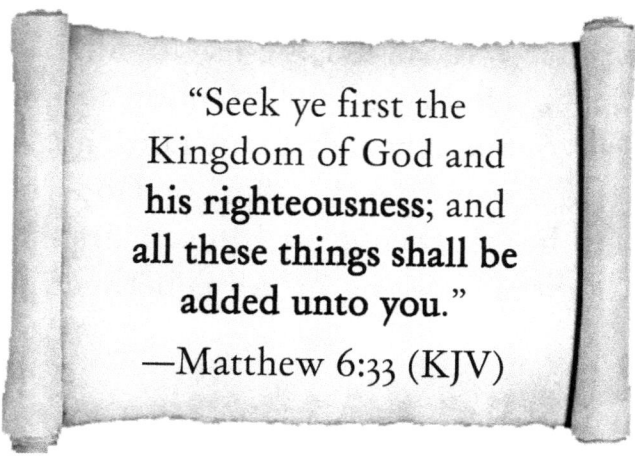

"Seek ye first the Kingdom of God and **his righteousness**; and **all these things shall be added unto you.**"
—Matthew 6:33 (KJV)

God promises us that after we are plugged in, we receive two gifts. The first gift we receive is **His righteousness**; His rightness; His greatness; His perfection. When we are plugged in, we receive the bonus gift of being powered by God's perfect holiness. This means we receive His truth and the truth shall set us free. His truth is His light filled with perfection; perfection of health, wealth, happiness, and wisdom. His light sets us free to live peacefully, lovingly, kindly, and joyfully, as well as boldly and courageously.

The second gift we receive is "all **these things** shall be added" unto us. What are THESE things? What THINGS? In the Holy Bible, God has left space in creation for each of us to write our own story, our own list of "things." Are we clear on our goals and

Connect First

desires for our life? What "things" do we currently desire in our life?

I challenge you to answer these questions for yourself:

Do I have a written mission statement for my life?

Am I clear on my goals and desires for my life?

Are my askings organized; these "things" in my life which I am calling in?

How much focus have I actually placed on the "things" of joy that I am allowing in?

Do I have a notebook full of ideas?

Am I journaling daily in an active proper journal from which I am calling out my askings to God?

God desires to give all these "things" to us, and He leaves "things" wide open. English professors teach us to please define the word "things" when we write. We are asked to replace "things" with descriptive nouns.

God has us fill in the blanks about "things". He privileges us with the opportunity to come up with a list of things and write them down. The idea is, like a parent, when our children come home we like to ask "What are YOU interested in? What are YOUR plans? What are YOUR desires?"

When we ask our children to choose a career or a focus at a university, we ask them what they are interested in and wish to study: "What is your heart's desire? All your hours will be used to do something. Have you thought about 'things' you are good at? 'Things' that come easily to you? What are 'things' that make you excited to jump out of bed in the morning?" First, take inventory: Have we recently answered all these questions for ourself? Now, let us answer these questions for ourself.

Connect First

What is your heart's desire?
_____
_____
_____

What are you good at?
_____
_____
_____

What comes easily to you?
_____
_____
_____

What excites you to jump out of bed in the morning?
_____
_____
_____

Connect To The Light

"All these things." Sit in contemplation and really think about what are these "things" that we are calling in and intentionally praying about. This is why I suggest that everybody has a journal and a pen with them **all the time**.

I actually recommend we have two or more journals, so we have one to write down our ideas and desires wherever we are; have one in our bag, in the car, at the kitchen table, on the bedside table.

To make our daily asking light and easy, Receive Joy created two beautiful journals: The *Daily Asking Journal* and the *Inspiration Notebook*.

The *Daily Asking Journal* helps us collect and compile all our askings and intentions of the day in one place. It also provides space to record our gratitude as well as our miracles and daily achievements.

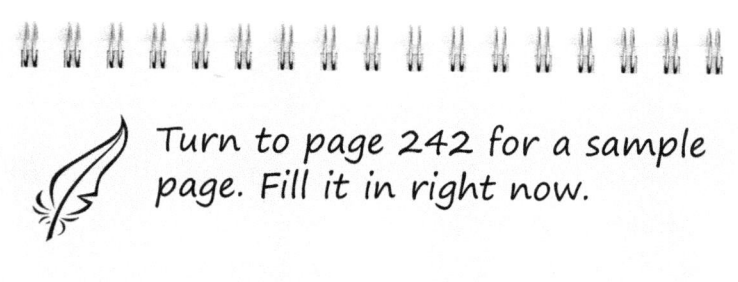

Turn to page 242 for a sample page. Fill it in right now.

The *Inspiration Notebook* is designed as a platform to create and record our inspirations, ideas, insights, goals, and plans.

Connect First

If we do happen to write a quick note in the car, at work, or elsewhere, tape it in the journals. Tape in all the scraps of paper, sticky notes, receipts holding your cool ideas, business cards, and sketches on napkins. Collect photos and pictures, magazine clippings, and other precious treasures gathered over the years and stick them in the journals. Blank note pages are included at the end of the journals allowing ample space.

When we "seek ye first the kingdom of God," we thank the Lord and praise Him.

> *Happy new day, God.*
> *Here I am. I thank You! I praise You! God, You are the source of light in my life. I recognize Your good that is abundant everywhere. Align our wills. I am holding my journal in my hands and I am praying to You. Oh God, bless me indeed and enlarge my territory. Keep Your hand upon me. You have my heart written down! Yes, I welcome in all these things to be added to my life.*
> *Thank You, Lord. I love You.*

Connect To The Light

Now God, His Universe, and I are on the same page knowing and creating the "things" of my heart. God is very easily and happily willing to add all these "things" and more. We can write "and more" on every page to leave it up to Him to happily surprise us with additional blessings. Today, God understands our thoughts and prayers. Tomorrow, we will add more. The next day, there will be even more. The next moment we think of new ideas, all this greatness expands to "and more."

One question often asked is, "Can I ask for other people?" Absolutely, as soon as we are good at asking for ourself. In this moment, the focus of this study is on ourself. Let us first practice asking and calling in for ourself, then speak the word over others to help them with their askings.

Once we have identified a desire, let us stay in our creation power until we achieve our desired goal. Let us keep our eyes on the victory.

One client who just recently started asking told me that she wrote down to receive a new refrigerator. Shortly after, she received one for free. However, it was defective; she laughed about it, edited her asking, and re-stated that she wishes for a clean, working refrigerator. Within the week she had a different one.

Connect First

At one of our Miracle Group meetings, several members were asking for new cars. The meeting was on Tuesday and we met the following Sunday for a party. Two members drove up with new white cars.

The first car story was inspired by Tuesday's lecture on staying in our creation dream a while longer and asking again, if we are yet waiting for the desired outcome. My friend told us on Tuesday that she wished for a new lease and a new car with the same payment options or more favorable than she had currently. When she went into the dealership the week before, she was told that she had to pay more as she was way over her allotted mileage. The next day after our meeting and after writing down her desired outcome, she went back again to the dealership. Miraculously, this time they immediately allowed her to trade in her old Mercedes for a newer model and she received an even better offer than she currently had.

Sometimes it is just a matter of **taking ourself away from the situation** and **putting our eyes back on the victory** before we return to the situation. This resets the whole receiving dynamic. Simply leaving the store and re-entering or taking a stroll around, may help to re-connect. My sister sometimes just turns around in a circle and asks again.

My mother went to a store recently and she was looking for a specific fabric. On her first diligent look in the fabric section, the fabric was yet to be found. Then, she went to the remnant table and also there the fabric was lacking. She remembered a story from one of the Miracle Group members who always finds the right size in the back of the store she worked at. Also, my mother had my voice in her head that I succeed leaving the store with exactly what I came to purchase. She decided to stay in her creation and take a second look, as everything can appear out of thin air instantly. She re-connected and sent a prayer to God and looked a second time. Then she said to herself, "I will leave with nine yards of the perfect fabric for $14 or less per yard." As she went to the fabric aisle the third time, she found the exact fabric with the exact yardage for the exact price she was looking for, knowing that it was only there the third time she looked.

Hearing about the leasing mileage experience inspired the second Miracle Group member driving up with a new car to formulate her asking for fun. She told us that she just went into a car dealership to meet the general manager referred to her by a friend, when she mentioned her fun exercise of creating something new. Her parameters were to have a more expensive car for the same monthly rate. As she was presented the offer, she said to the general manager, "The numbers shall be much more favorable if you wish

Connect First

to sell me a new car today." She went outside, and the general manager came after her and asked her what it will take for her to buy the car that day. Being honest with herself she said she will consider purchasing the car if the monthly rate was a maximum of $20 more than her current payment. When the manager came back, he was really excited about the offer he presented to her. As the offer met her terms, she gladly accepted. Another parameter on her list was to own the car and have it paid off within a year. God also made this happen miraculously through an extra financial blessing which came her way a year later.

Are we clear on our goals, our "things," our desires, and the goodness for our life? Clarity begins by collecting data on ourself and having a mission statement. This is exactly what the exercises on the following pages are designed to help us accomplish. Let us live a purposeful life by design.

Chapter 3

THE GRAND DOORS OF MY LIFE

We are all born with gifts, strengths, and talents. Let us be aware of the talents we are gifted with and use them. Everyone came into this existence with a divine mission. Everyone has a definite purpose for their life. It is important to take the time to acknowledge and embrace our personal purpose.

Before we start to collect data on ourself and then write our mission statement, let us take a moment and do a revealing exercise.

The Grand Doors Of My Life

Close your eyes and picture in front of you a beautiful set of grand doors.

Behind these doors are all your dreams and desires. The space beyond these doors is filled with light. It is full of goodness, glory, comfort, and happiness.

Now, open the doors. The grand doors to your perfect life swing open.

And as the doors now are being opened, our smiling Creator greets you on the other side, saying "welcome to the abundant, beautiful life we created together."

Now feel with your heart: What is revealed behind the doors?

What are your life's dreams and desires?

What do you see first?

Connect To The Light

What is the landscape like? Is there a forest or are you at the beach? Is there a river or a fountain? Do you see buildings?

Who is there with you? Is your family there? Are your friends around? Visualize the people that are there with you. Or is it just you alone with nature?

Do you see animals? Are there birds and butterflies? Are there pets with you?

Is it warm? Is it cool?

What time of the day is it? Is the sun shining? Are the stars glowing? Is it day and night at the same time?

What else do you notice? What colors are greeting you? What smells and sounds are greeting you? Are they sounds of nature? Are they sounds from some other place?

The Grand Doors Of My Life

BEHIND THE GRAND DOORS OF MY LIFE

_____

_____

_____

_____

_____

_____

_____

_____

_____

_____

_____

_____

_____

Connect To The Light

When the doors of your life open, is there a career on the other side? What activities are you engaging in? Is there singing? Dancing? Is there giving? Is there receiving?

What do you look like? What are you wearing?

Are you happy? Is there a smile on your face and joy in your heart?

Are you calm? Are you relaxed and peaceful?

Do you feel a sense of accomplishment and worthiness?

Do you love what you see?

Make any adjustments you desire in this ideal version of your life and the ideal you.

Stay here for a while and experience what it feels like! Be in the expanse of all that is. Call forth whatever you wish to step into.

The Grand Doors Of My Life

BEHIND THE GRAND DOORS OF MY LIFE

_____
_____
_____
_____
_____
_____
_____
_____
_____
_____
_____
_____
_____
_____
_____

Connect To The Light

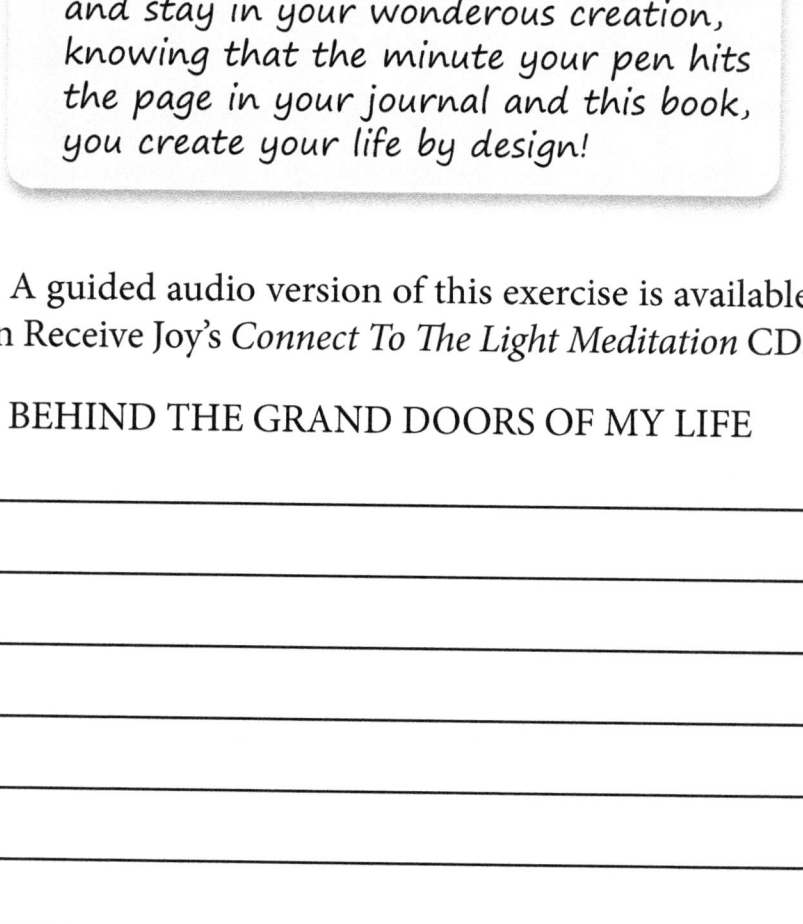

Decide to stay with the doors wide open, and then step in and live in that space.

I call you back to open your eyes and stay in your wonderous creation, knowing that the minute your pen hits the page in your journal and this book, you create your life by design!

A guided audio version of this exercise is available on Receive Joy's *Connect To The Light Meditation* CD.

BEHIND THE GRAND DOORS OF MY LIFE

_____

_____

_____

_____

_____

_____

The Grand Doors Of My Life

BEHIND THE GRAND DOORS OF MY LIFE

_____

_____

_____

_____

_____

_____

_____

_____

_____

_____

_____

_____

_____

_____

Connect To The Light

BEHIND THE GRAND DOORS OF MY LIFE

The Grand Doors Of My Life

What are we calling in? What have we divinely called in to set up this wonderful space and time that is our life? Is it so exiting and inviting that we can call it our oasis? Are we excited to enter into this grand creation? As we step in, are we smiling and is our heart beating with joy, laughter, and goodness?

Is my life everything I wish it to be? Sometimes, we wish to retire from what we created so far in our life. Are we yet to match our dreams and desires with our reality? Let us take the first step by consciously creating the life of our dreams within the Grand Doors we have recently opened and stepped into, so that we create a clear image of what our life shall transform into in our current existence to truly satisfy us.

Everything we see beyond the Grand Doors shall be scripted in our journal and then via the very power in this Universe it will appear in our life. Let us decide to be excited to welcome in and enter the life of our dreams.

We may repeat this exercise as often as we wish. Is there anything we see that requires active change? If this is the first time that this exercise is done, we may face the question of what we truly wish to see as the doors open. This is just the beginning. We may only see the first entry room of our life, and there are many more rooms waiting to be designed. There is room after room and space after space beyond this first vision that we have. Day by day, let us create additional areas. There can be a children's area and a beautiful retirement area, a garden area and a nature area with animals. There might be fields of green grass with little flowers. There might be fields of lavender and fields of sunflowers. There can be areas where inventions are being created. There is a love area where people gather to encourage and share love with one another. There is a praise area where there is song and worship. There is a miracle area where miracles are performed in every moment, and God is continually praised. Let us step over the threshold into our awe-inspiring life and experience the next miracle. We can see it and we can feel it, and our Creator is here, still smiling. This is our opportunity to actively create, create, create, and to find joy in our creation.

As we decide to stay in our dream with the doors wide open and live in this space, we know that the moment our pen hits the page in our journal, the next area is created. As we choose to stay in our dream, we see our beautiful new creation expanding before us. Let us dedicate time to play in our own creation with joy and happiness.

Along our path of studying, working, marriage,

raising children, tending to love ones, and more, we might have to remind ourself over and over what beauty lies beyond our own doors. With constant contemplation, meditation, and focus, we visualize our own heart's desires more clearly. We know that **what we focus on we will receive more of**. Thus, **focus well** and focus often.

FIVE MINUTE COUCH TIME

Let us take five minutes for ourself daily and ask some very important questions. We call this focus exercise **Five Minute Couch Time**. Let us sit down in creative contemplation. This time is designated for self-growth and realization while we place the rest of our world on hold. We may ponder questions and welcome solutions from God during this Couch Time. Examples of things to ponder are:

- ♥ I am less than satisfied with this situation. What do I really wish to have happen instead? What do I desire to be different?

> - ♥ What is the next space or room of my life I am ready to create beyond my Grand Doors? Is there a new design for my career, my family, my study, my health, my wealth, my happiness or something else? What does this look like? What are the details within this particular space or room?
> - ♥ Why do I have an emotion less than love when I think of a certain person, event, or place? How can that change?
> - ♥ What is my life's mission? Am I on my life's path toward my mission?

I have a friend who comes to town frequently and then we meet to catch up. I met him about two years ago, when he attended the Miracle Group with his mother. At that time, he was on a quest for answers to improve his life and self-assurance. He was blessed by, and received clarification, through the information provided in *Ask And You Shall Receive*, as well as our conversations and self-reflection.

The first time we met for dinner, I encouraged him to write down his three major askings for the next few months, so that he can incorporate new positive energy and beliefs in his life.

When we met again, he was full of excitement, and before we even had a chance to sit down he said, "Everything we wrote down last time came to be. Exactly as we wrote it! I will fill you in on the details." After he excitedly shared the details with me, I urged him to write down even more for the coming months. Again, when we met, every single asking transpired. Since our first meeting he grew tremendously using the Power of Prayer and Asking. Once he learned to ask for his daily petitions, he was ready to open up his mind to ask for bigger miracles and even things he was yet to be aware of to ask for.

Chapter 4

COLLECTING DATA ON MYSELF

Asking and answering questions about ourself enables us to gain an understanding of who we truly are. To create and write out a Personal Divine Mission Statement, let us take an inventory and continue to discover what the Grand Doors of our beautiful space revealed.

Collecting Data On Myself

 Start with an awareness of what you enjoy. The following questions will help guide you to re-discover yourself.

Pick up your pen and circle your answers. You may also circle both possibilities if fitting. Write your answers in this book.

Are you an indoor person or an outdoor person?

Do you enjoy living in the city or outside the city?

Do you prefer the ocean or the mountains?

Do you prefer a beach house or a cabin in the woods?

Do you like warm weather or cold weather?

Sunshine, rain, or snow?

Connect To The Light

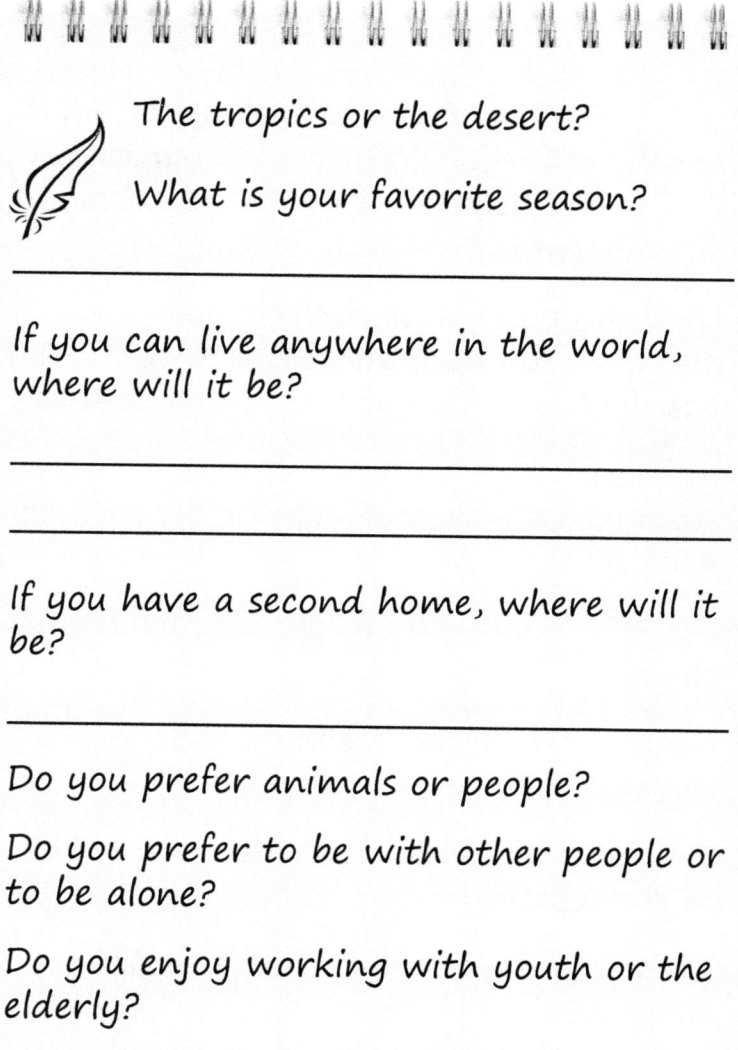

The tropics or the desert?

What is your favorite season?

_____

If you can live anywhere in the world, where will it be?

_____

_____

If you have a second home, where will it be?

_____

Do you prefer animals or people?

Do you prefer to be with other people or to be alone?

Do you enjoy working with youth or the elderly?

Collecting Data On Myself

What talents do you have?
_____
_____
_____
_____
_____

What are your hobbies?
_____
_____
_____

What sports do you enjoy?
_____
_____
_____

Connect To The Light

 Do you prefer music or dancing?

Do you like listening to music or playing music yourself?

Do you enjoy taking pictures or making home movies?

Do you prefer reading or watching movies?

Do you enjoy learning or teaching?

Are you a seminar enthusiast?

Do you enjoy making or eating food?

Cooking or baking?

Do you enjoy spa treatments?

Are you the giver or receiver of spa treatments?

Do you prefer to give time or money to a charitable cause?

Collecting Data On Myself

What types of charities are you attracted to?
_____
_____
_____

What are you good at?
_____
_____
_____
_____
_____

What truly makes you happy?
_____
_____
_____

Connect To The Light

What do you do for fun?
_____
_____
_____
_____

What do you do for hours and it seems like only minutes?
_____
_____

What causes you to jump out of bed energetically and enthusiastically in the morning?
_____
_____
_____

This is your passion!

Collecting Data On Myself

Remember, **our life's purpose is our greatest joy**! It is why we came into this existence to do this particular greatness. We shall go forth in greatness and wonder, and live wonderful lives—lives full of wonder. Now we can utilize a Five Minute Couch Time and ask:

> *What will it take for me to feel like my life is full of wonder?*
> _____
> _____
> _____
> _____
> _____

The questions above, and those following, are all designed to encourage our imagination and cause us to discover ourself. Let us continue to think productive thoughts for this part of our life, and approach our life pro-actively. As our reasons to do things change, we have to change with them. Life is continually asking us "What is next?"

Connect To The Light

What is next for me?

What does the next stage of my life look like?

Collecting Data On Myself

Does it require change?
Yes   No   (Circle your answer)

Does it involve growing, expanding, downsizing?
(Circle your answer)

Will you require encouragement?
Yes   No   (Circle your answer)

Are you keeping your mind wide open?
Yes   No   (Circle your answer)

Let us journal a whole page whenever a change is upon us. Maybe we are starting a new relationship or desire to enter one. Or perhaps it is time for a new job or to plan a vacation. Each and every experience deserves to be scripted about first. **Visualize, define, ask.**

When one of our Miracle Group members was ready to move to our area full time, he required that his house in Chicago be sold and a new job secured for him here. Once he was ready to release his house in Chicago and commit to his new life here, he received offers for his house. He arrived and began his job search. He applied everywhere and waited for replies. When he stopped applying and instead sat down in contemplation, he asked himself what career is fun for him. He recalled that solar energy always was of great interest to him. However, previously when he looked into solar energy jobs in this area, the industry was too new. After this self-exploration, he went online and to his surprise, he found five thriving companies. He applied to four and received a job interview the very next day. Once he was true to himself, specified what is fun to him, and what he is really excited about, everything started flowing in his favor.

At the same Miracle Group meeting, another member shared how she miraculously received an email with a job offer out of the blue. When she read the email, she saw herself fitting the job description perfectly. Out of curiosity she did apply and was invited for an interview. During the interview she felt welcomed by the staff. Upon reflection, she realized she might be ready to work with new, exciting, more positive people. The new belief pattern she recently had grown into, valued self-worth and included being worthy of God's love and almighty power. To receive a new job and to let go of the old one, she simply accepted that she deserved all aspects of happiness, including a fun and satisfying job with exciting, positive co-workers.

Questioning ourself and collecting data on ourself sparks our creative juices to continually and actively create what is next; the next room, the next project, the next personal greatness.

I may discover that I am really an outdoor person and then I ask myself, "Are my talents and my hobbies doing things outside? If I am an indoor person, am I spending most of my time inside? Am I spending my time doing what I love? Does our current life align with our answers? Am I using the greatness that I have to do what I really desire?"

These questions can be answered right in this book. Write all over this book. Our answers can be crossed out and rewritten as many times as desired.

Our life's creation is a masterpiece that is continually being edited. **Write, write, write!**

We are continuing to collect data on ourself. Let us now collect data on our personal happiness. Let us write a Fun List. This list contains "things" that make our heart sing today. Let us write down every activity that brings us joy, that we are excited about, that makes us jump in our car and drive to it. It may be an exercise class or an inspiration class.

Connect To The Light

It may be a Bible Study, a Miracle Group meeting, or tea with a friend. If that's what makes our heart sing this year, then that is what we include on our Fun List.

Why do we make a Fun List? Having a Fun List helps us engage in fun activities for ourself. Some of us require a reminder of what now at this stage of our life is fun to us. In our thirties, different things are fun to us than in our teens or twenties. Maybe we were a passionate biker when we were 25, and our knees now wish to do some other activity. Every stage of our life requires a new Fun List. We have to update ourself. We have to update our lists and check our heart today. What is fun today? What is fun in this season of my life?

If we have a spouse, what new things at our age do we enjoy doing together? If we have a boyfriend or girlfriend, what is fun and exciting for both of us?

Start collecting data on your personal happiness. Write your own "Fun List"! This list contains things that make your heart sing.

Collecting Data On Myself

MY FUN LIST

Connect To The Light

How can we implement more personal fun into our life?

For example, if we discover that gardening is our joy, and we live in a condo, we can buy a pot to plant seeds or put flowers in. A "garden" can be as simple as a pot. A single flower can be our garden joy.

Let us take action with a simple step. Start with the focused intent of a small idea and let it grow and grow and grow. Taking actions is similar to planting seeds. Every idea, dream, or thought is a seed. We grow that thought; we add to it, we pray over it, we have conversations about it, we share it with family, friends, and colleagues, we research it, we collect information. To gain momentum, let us do the smallest little movement. Let us grow our Fun List continually, add to it, and most importantly: **live the fun!**

People with the same vibrational energy flock together. We are drawn to, and we attract people that are like us. This is why we join groups. There may be people and groups in our life that we somehow have vibrated with for a long time, that were fun to be part of and to play with. Maybe we used to go out with friends who do certain activities we have outgrown now that we prefer to live by design. As our values, life design, and self-vision evolve, the groups we are drawn to may change.

Let us consider a really important point: Are the people we spend time with, people who engage in our old behavior or people who engage in our new behavior? If we take the old energy field and we keep playing in it, even with new ideas and enlightenment, we are still in the old energy field with the same old energy people. Today, we are taking inventory of ourself and actively choosing our new beautiful life. Let us attract new people into our life and make new friends to enjoy the activities we are currently excited about.

Further, it may have been joyful for some time of our life to be part of a particular group of people. Or maybe it was less than joyful, yet we still hung out with them. We outgrow people and groups. Even if they stepped up their game ten notches, if we have stepped up our game 100 notches, we are ready to move on and play with the people who are in the 100-notch category from now on. We also allow the old group to stay where they are. It works for them and that is okay. Let us move on and graduate completely, like we graduated from high school and college. It is alright to outgrow people. We outgrew our baby socks, we outgrew our high school socks. It is time to sort through and clean up our sock drawer and have only the socks inside that fit us now. Let us give ourself permission to move on. Change means when the Grand Doors open up, we are walking out of something and into something greater. Let us move into and stay in our greatness!

The idea is, if we live by design, and we have designed our life to grow and change, then we shall let ourself stay in this growth. Let the head be aligned with the heart in growth. Our heart will lead us to the right friends to spend time with.

Be a new creation. If we wish to be new, and to increase our vibrational field, let us play with people who have a strong, beautiful, joyful, cheerful, enlightened, encouraging, divinely focused energy field. Let us **take responsibility for our own life and find joy in it**.

If we are ordering a pizza, we tell the person taking our order our exact desires. Do we like cheese crust? Do we prefer extra toppings? Are we a meat lover? Do we prefer only vegetables? Often, in our life's pizza parlor, we just walk in, sit down, and talk to our friends, and because they have already ordered a pizza, we accept their order. When that pizza is served, we end up eating someone else's pizza, even if we honestly prefer a different pizza for ourself. Let

Collecting Data On Myself

us always order our own pizza with all the delicious toppings we desire.

Now let us further investigate what our life by design looks like. Let us focus on where we are heading. Defining who I am and my ideal self is a transformational experience. These lists allow us to think about ourself, take inventory, and then envision what else is beyond the Grand Doors. Where am I right now? To reach our desired destination, we have to accept where we are starting from today.

On the following page, create a second list of "Who I Am" and then a third list of "My Ideal Self." This list contains every attribute of who you are ready to be. Continually add to your lists.

Connect To The Light

WHO I AM

Collecting Data On Myself

MY IDEAL SELF

Connect To The Light

Let us welcome in what we have right now and celebrate every aspect of who we are in this moment, because the first step to a life in connection is self-love and acceptance.

> *I love myself. I love myself. I love myself! I love my God. I am the child of the most high God. I have His creation power within me. I am connected to God. I am harnessed on. I am taking inventory of what is right now. And then I am building a life by design by stating in positive words the exact creation that I shall be, because I have designed my life connected to God. I know my ideal life is already in existence.*

Now, return to the lists above and remember to list everything you love about yourself and compliments you have received.

Where do I wish to be? Our ideal self is the target

Collecting Data On Myself

that we allow ourself to achieve—our life by design. If our ideal self weighs 120 pounds, then on the "My Ideal Self" list it may state "120-pound beautiful woman." However, many people write "I'm *going to be* ... this way," "I'm *going to lose* 'something.'" The Universe only grows and expands. How much does the Universe ever *"lose"*? Zero! Remember, the Universe *"needs and wants for nothing."* God's Universe already has and contains everything. If we are *"going to get"* something or *"want"* something, the Quantum Field allows us to *"keep going and going"* and *"wanting and wanting,"* *"trying to get"* and *"needing"* instead of receiving it into our life. Let us move on from the *"wanting state"* and declare that all is already here. We desire to reach specific goals – name them! Let us write exactly that beautiful ideal self into existence.

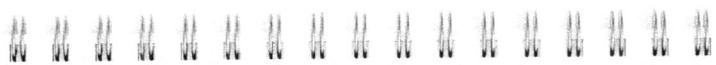

Look over your lists again and if necessary change your words to present tense. Use definite, positive statements about yourself.

Now, God and His Universe know exactly how to assist us.

Connect To The Light

When writing the lists, think about all the categories in your life and know where you are right now, and where you wish to be. The following questions help you evaluate your current self and start designing your ideal self. Feel free to add to your lists. The answers to these questions may spark additional insight. If you require more space, use the note pages in the back of the book.

Spirituality:

Are you connected to God?

Do you have absolute faith?

Do you believe that you are worthy of God's love?

Are you experiencing His light?

Do you believe that when Jesus died for us on the cross, He did a complete work so that now we can live to rejoice?

Do you read your Bible?

Collecting Data On Myself

 Are you actively praising and worshipping God?

Do you pray daily?

Do you have a prayer partner?

Physical Body:

What does perfect health look like for you?

Are you eating healthy food?

What is the ideal weight for your body?

What is your ideal exercise routine, and how many times a week do you exercise?

Do you have a workout buddy?

What is your desired hair color?

How do you wish to dress—for business and casual?

Are you giving your body permission and time to relax?

Do you meditate?

Connect To The Light

Thoughts:

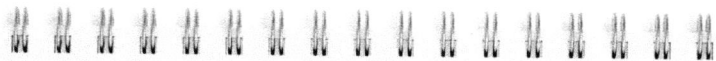

Are all your thoughts positive?

Are there any beliefs that require an update?

Are your beliefs your own?

Are your beliefs supporting your greatness?

Words:

Do you speak positive encouraging uplifting words at all times?

Are there still words and phrases in your vocabulary that require substitution?

Emotions:

How do you feel? Is this how you wish to feel?

What feelings do you wish to experience more often?

Collecting Data On Myself

Are you happy?

Do you feel worthy and deserving?

Do you feel loved?

How long does it take you to let go of an emotion that is less than love?

Strengths and Talents:

Do you know what you are good at?

Do you know your strengths? What are they?

Do you know your talents? What are they?

Have you taken any personality tests? What were the results?

Relationships:

Do you have a personal relationship with God?

Do you still have to forgive yourself and others?

Connect To The Light

Is everyone around you uplifting?

Are you excited about everyone you interact with?

Do you give yourself permission to enjoy being alone?

How many close friends do you have or wish to have?

How can you improve existing relationships?

Are there any current relationships you have to pass on?

What kind of intimate relationship with a partner do you desire (single, happily married, married with children)? What does this ideal relationship look like?

Do you have an accountability partner?

Collecting Data On Myself

Material manifestations:

Do you live where you wish to live (country, state, city, house)?

Do you drive the car you are absolutely thrilled to drive?

Do you own everything you wish to possess?

Are there things you wish to let go of?

Do you feel organized?

Do you know where everything is?

Wealth and Finances:

Do you know the number that it will take to support you for the rest of your life?

Do you consider yourself rich?

Do you have positive feelings toward wealthy people?

Do you have an abundance mindset and empowering beliefs?

Connect To The Light

 Is there anything from your past that may be holding you back from your financial freedom?

Are you continually educating yourself about wealth?

Are you resourceful?

Career:

Are you on your desired career path?

Is your work fun?

Do you thoroughly enjoy the people you work with?

Is it time for a new work creation?

Do you use your strengths and talents?

Are you receiving the proper compensation?

Collecting Data On Myself

Activities:

Do you engage in your favorite activities regularly?

What activities do you wish to add to your schedule?

What activities do you wish to drop from your schedule?

What tasks can you delegate to free yourself?

What languages do you wish to speak?

What places do you wish to visit?

What is fun for you now?

Are you excited to wake up and start your day?

Goals:

What goals accomplished in the next 90 days will make you most happy?

Connect To The Light

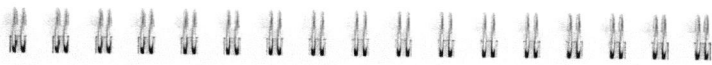

What goals accomplished in the next year will make you most happy?

What goals accomplished by the end of your earthly existence will make you most happy and fulfilled?

"Each one should test their own actions. Then they can take pride in themselves alone, without comparing themselves to someone else,"
—Galatians 6:4 (NIV)

Chapter 5

MY DIVINE MISSION

Now that we know what excites us, it is the perfect time to learn how to write our mission statement.

Connect To The Light

Review your lists: Who Am I, My Ideal Self, and My Fun List and circle the top one to five most important words that describe you. Write them here:

_____

_____

_____

_____

Choose one or two action words that describe you best. Write them here:

_____

_____

My Divine Mission

Formulate your mission statement using your chosen words.

The following easy format will help you:

"My divine mission is to

_____

_____

_____

_____

for/with myself and others."

For example:

"My divine mission is to give and receive joy and experience health for myself and others through rediscovering the truth."

"My divine mission is to share happiness with the Universe."

Connect To The Light

This is your current mission statement. It may be edited often. As interests change and our focus shifts, it is okay to have a working version of our mission statement and change it as often as we desire.

My three words that describe me and are my greatest fun in one of my rooms, beyond my beautiful doors where my creator and I play all day long, are: **Happiness**, **Health**, and **Wealth**. I formulated a sentence out of these three words.

> My divine mission is to share **joy**, **health**, and **wealth** in this world through **resetting** myself and others to God's divine perfection that we already are.

For me, **health** is my big word, then my action word is **resetting**. I use biofeedback equipment and light and sound therapies to accomplish this. To balance and energize the body's vibrational patterns, I combine light and sound to reset. Remember, health is within us already because we are harnessed to God. I simply measure the body's frequencies and reset

My Divine Mission

them. I tune and harmonize frequencies in myself and others similar to a reset switch on our power outlets. We just push the red button and the circuit resets. Sometimes we have to go to the circuit breaker and flip the switch to reset the circuit.

I en**joy** being happy and I feel that mastering **wealth** is part of our daily life. The better I manage my finances the more I can share.

First, we check that we are plugged in to the active power source. Let us reset ourself to our greatness. Let us start by writing down our mission.

Even children can practice formulating their divine mission. My nephew loves to build with Legos and his mission is as simple as:

> My divine mission is to be a great builder.

My niece's mission statement is short and fun. She has one word: Happiness.

Connect To The Light

> *My divine mission is to share happiness with the Universe.*

It is amazing; she just loves happiness. She can add, "The happier I am, the more happiness I can share with the Universe."

We also spent some time on her Fun List. I asked her what she desired to do right now. As a young person in her early twenties she said, "I just desire to work at Disney." I said, "Do you know that Disneyland is known as 'The Happiest Place On Earth' and the slogan for Magic Kingdom is 'The Most Magical Place On Earth?' Of course you wish to work there! If your divine mission is to share happiness, I think working at the happiest place on Earth will be ideal!" It is beautiful that Disney created a happiness theme as their mission statement.

The exercise was really fun with her and she actually did a happy internship at the happiest place on Earth.

My Divine Mission

One word that shall be in everyone's mission statement is "myself." Remember to include "myself." As I have been doing this over the years, I have noticed that people write their mission statement and it is often only written about "others." I comment, "Well, that is amazing. Who is the one doing all this for others? Where are you in the mission statement?"

Who is doing all of this greatness? It is us! We are the witness to our own life. If we are x in the equation $x+y=z$, and we remove the x, the equation is less than complete. Let us include the x, ourself, in our mission statement.

For example, one mission statement says, "My divine mission is to help people by building wells to provide drinking water in their villages."

First, we have to develop our life to have the time, finances, and wherewithal so that we can then build wells for people and provide them with drinking water. The more we improve ourself, the earlier we put our air masks on ourself, the better our life is and our ability to assist the people around us. In this example, a more powerful mission statement is:

Connect To The Light

> *My divine mission is to grow myself and my wealth so that I can help people by building wells to provide drinking water in their villages.*

With our divine mission, we are defining and declaring our current purpose in life. When we investigate our own being, we keep ourself in the present. Let us strengthen ourself so that we can help others. First, we help ourself, then we are able to help others even better. The more we help ourself the more valuable we are to others.

We allow lots of variety in our life. Throughout the day we are playing different roles: The role of a husband or wife, the role of a parent, the role of a sister or brother, the role of an entrepreneur or employee. People around us require us to be fully engaged in our roles, which we are only able to do when we take care of our mind, body, and spirit first. As an employee, our employer loves for us to show up healthy, happy, and whole. We are most productive when we are healthy, happy, whole, and able to focus.

My Divine Mission

Let us answer the questions now.

Am I focused?

Do I have a life mission?

Do I have a current personal mission statement?

Have I defined my life's purpose?

Am I enjoying my life?

Let us answer the questions now.

If you are yet to answer the questions above, grab your pen and start writing.

Place your divine mission where you can see it and be constantly reminded of it.

Memorize it!

Connect To The Light

We came into this awesome world filled with love and light. Now we are here with the opportunity to **experience** this **love and light** for ourself, and to **share it with others**.

My Divine Mission

My divine mission is _____
_____
_____
_____
_____
_____
_____
_____
_____
_____
_____
_____
_____
_____

Chapter 6

FEEL THE CONNECTION

We are truly connected to God when our heart feels His presence. The feeling of connection may vary for each and every one of us. It might be:

- ♥ A knowing as if someone is surrounding us with love

- ♥ A warm comforting "gut feeling"

- ♥ A lead, a nudge, an urge, an instinct, or an intuition

- ♥ A sense of security

- ♥ A new idea or a divine inspiration

- ♥ Goosebumps

- ♥ The thrilling sensation of hair standing up

Feel The Connection

- ♥ A whisper or a voice talking
- ♥ Messages through nature or other beings with a confirmation
- ♥ A sense of belonging
- ♥ A feeling of comforting peace and calmness
- ♥ A feeling of elation
- ♥ A change in the atmosphere
- ♥ Behavior and words coming through us as we wonder how and why

When we have an idea, a hunch, or a nudge, are we trusting that these leads are from the divine or from our mind? When we follow our immediate feelings, our first thoughts and intuitions, our path is made straight. Let us **trust our intuitive thoughts and feelings**. Our "gut feeling" is our gauge that allows us to be led toward something or away from it. Our gut feelings are a gift. They allow us sensitivity to what we are experiencing. We can use two simple phrases to describe our major gut feelings: Either something feels good and we welcome more of it and move toward it, or we feel the opposite. When change is required, we move away from it. Another way to put it is, "This is my blessing" or "This is someone else's blessing."

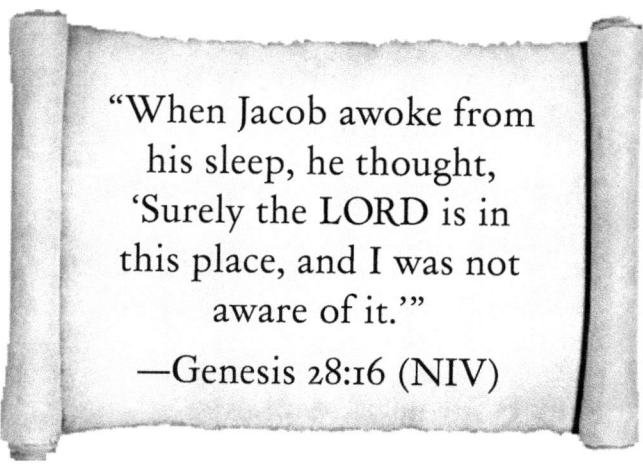

"When Jacob awoke from his sleep, he thought, 'Surely the LORD is in this place, and I was not aware of it.'"
—Genesis 28:16 (NIV)

Surely the Lord is in this place. Jacob sensed it. He felt the connection. Surely the Lord is in us as well. Let us be conscious of God's presence, listen for his direction, and use His guidance. When we are connected to God, we have the opportunity to tap into **higher knowing**, a higher state of being aware and informed. Let us resonate with this higher knowing, this all-knowing, this true and higher enlightenment. All-knowing is an absolute feeling of confidence that this will come to be. Our mind thinks, yet our divine self knows. Our mind considers by conscious reasoning, while knowing is received intuitively.

We recognize that we are in our state of all-knowing when we have **a feeling of euphoric confidence**. We are drawn toward this assurance in confidence and certainty. There is such a peace within us that this is meant to be and it will come to be. We know that this is right and we do everything in confidence, while the world falls away as we go forth.

We have times in our life when we live by our knowing. I, and I alone, am ready to stand my ground. We are intently steadfast and sure in our knowing that all is well even if God is our only ally. It is okay that God is our only ally as we joyfully venture forward on our mission. When we are in our knowing, we accomplish things beyond the normal. Staying in our knowing conserves energy and connects to supernatural energy resources. When we have tapped into God's Power and have increased our focused consciousness, only then can we create more in a year than we can accomplish by drifting through our entire life with lack of purpose. **We are practicing focused consciousness** when we are directly on our path that we called forth. We follow our heart and we are in alignment with God.

Let us allow ourself to be directed by our higher knowing. Whatever we do, have, or be, make sure to utilize our all-knowing. When we are connected and penetrated with our higher knowing, **we instinctively know what actions are right** for who we are, and every task gives us joy and a sense of fulfilment.

Connect To The Light

Think of a time when you lived your all-knowing. You felt confident. You knew all was well and everything will turn out alright. You were intuitively aware. You were instinctively informed. Feel the feeling. Go into that place of knowing and feel it in your heart. Feel how powerful you were in that moment. Feel the euphoria.

Practice being in your all-knowing. Anchor this beautiful feeling in and feel it daily.

Declare yourself in your higher knowing. Say your name and declare

"I, (name), am in my higher knowing. I know. Thank you, so be it."

Speak this statement out loud as often as it takes you to resonate truthfully with it and feel its solidity. Feel the certainty throughout your body.

Feel The Connection

Many people told me the story of how they met their spouses and how it felt divinely inspired, and they just knew. For example, one Miracle Group member who just recently moved into town told me that her husband of a year knew exactly that she was the one for him when he picked her up at the airport for their second date. A woman I met at the gym said that she saw a white light around her husband when she met him the first time and her world appeared in slow motion.

Another story is from a friend in her eighties. In her late teens, she went to a dance at a teacher convention with a girlfriend. Before the evening began, she prayed: "Please God, remember me and send me a husband." They had a good time looking down from the balcony over the dance floor when her girlfriend recognized someone she knew. My friend decided to go to the bathroom and she prayed again, "Dear God, there are so many handsome men, please find me one here." When she came out of the bathroom her girlfriend introduced her to her acquaintance and his friend. There was a standstill like in the movies at that time, and a voice said, "Here he is." She felt excited meeting the friend, yet at the same time she was reasoning with God: "Really, God? I thought my husband will be taller."

Connect To The Light

In this moment, she heard a voice: "Next time!" She knew immediately that she will be married twice in her lifetime. Her first husband passed away after 46 years of having a happy life together. A few years later, she is now remarried to a man who is taller indeed.

When we question a part of our life, we may ask ourself if this circumstance is right for us, or if we shall move away from it. Let us also **concentrate on the feeling we have when we think about it**. Do we feel absolute certainty and do we have the same confident feeling we had when we thought about something that was right for us? Now, we have the answer. When we feel certainty, we are connected. Anything that is less than that feeling of certainty is temporary. Does our thinking overshadow our feelings?

Let our heart teach us. Align the head (thinking) with the heart (feeling) and allow our God-given knowing to be present. Feel the strength of the heart center. Let us trust our heart. Feel the knowing. Consciously work with it. We know what it is to know in complete confidence. We know when we know. Once we know, start acting accordingly. It feels right to take action from this place of knowing. Act from this place of knowing and do it again and again; this is faith in action. **Exercise steadfast faith!**

When my oldest daughter returned for her Junior Year to the Savannah College of Art and Design in Georgia, she required an apartment. We gave ourselves a two-day visit to Savannah to rent a place. We already looked online and set up a few viewings upon our arrival. All the apartments shown to us had yet to excite us. To stimulate our asking mood, we went to my daughter's favorite coffee shop, which is next to her favorite purple house and the park. We took out pen and paper and made a list of everything the right apartment shall have:

- ♥ Enough room to paint on large canvases
- ♥ Parking for her van
- ♥ Close to the coffee shop and health food store
- ♥ Close to the park
- ♥ Close to the purple house
- ♥ $1,000/month maximum rent
- ♥ A ten-month lease for the duration of the year's classes

Connect To The Light

- ♥ Lots of windows
- ♥ Living alone
- ♥ Washer and dryer
- ♥ Hardwood floors
- ♥ Newer building
- ♥ Fresh smell inside
- ♥ Everything clean

On the way to the coffee shop we saw a sign from a rental agency in the front yard of a building. We called the realtor and read her our parameter list and told her what we are looking for. She said, she had the right place for us and it was located a block from the coffee shop. We made an appointment for a showing a few hours later, as she was attending other clients. We used the time to check out the exact building and neighborhood. When we viewed the apartment, we loved it and it did fit all criteria except one. I signed a 12-month lease the next day and my daughter enjoyed her time in her apartment; even so, I told God that 10 months is all the rent I wish to pay.

When nine and a half months were up, she moved home for the summer. I had this conversation with

Feel The Connection

God: "Remember my 10-month lease, God. Nine and a half months ago I asked You for a 10-month lease even though I signed a 12-month lease." Two days later, the same realtor called me asking if she might refund my security deposit and terminate the 12-month lease as she had a new renter that was ready to move into the apartment immediately. God is very precise. He delivers when we require it most. Remember, He often delivers at the last minute. **When we have placed an asking on His altar and LEAVE IT THERE for Him, we can have absolute faith and trust that our asking has been fulfilled**, even when the reasoning mind, which we call our intellect, continually calls us to snatch our askings back off the altar.

When we are confident and secure in our knowing, we experience the unification of our true potential and our true self. Please remember, everything we are is already within us. Like a seed, all the information is contained inside us. An apple seed grows into an apple tree. An olive seed grows into an olive tree. Let us acknowledge what kind of seed we are and live a life of true alignment with our unique divine greatness. We are the seed of God. He put all the answers already in us. Realize the magnitude of what we inherently know already. Remember and rediscover the truth within. Our purpose is a part of us from the beginning. Let us be clear with ourself—

Connect To The Light

we have all the resources for a fulfilled life within us. We hold His wisdom, which God ordained before the beginning of time.

> "He has saved us and called us to a holy life—not because of anything we have done but because of his own purpose and grace. This grace was given us in Christ Jesus before the beginning of time,"
> —II Timothy 1:9 (NIV)

As children we saw everything clearly, we followed our hunches, and considered our own happiness until we placed perceived worldly expectations on ourself. We were born following our intuition, which simply means to be taught from within. Then we decided to turn from our own internal knowing. Outside influences lead us to deviate with messages such as:

- ♥ *There are enough starving artists in this world*
- ♥ *Oh, computer programmers are a dime a dozen*

Feel The Connection

- ♥ *You'll never make it*
- ♥ *We don't have the money*
- ♥ *We expect you to take over the family business*
- ♥ *We need a doctor, a lawyer, and an accountant in our family*
- ♥ *There is no money in teaching*

We have all heard many of these phrases or similar ones. Let us all be encouraging to each other and trust that we each know our gifts best, and are able to create opportunities for ourself to flourish and live our unique greatness in our own way. Whatever we are—we are already excellent!

Let us ask ourself: Are we stuck living in the illusion of *"problems"* and *"victimhood"* coming up with *"excuses"* and handing out *"blame,"* or are we living a solution-oriented, purpose-driven life? It is our choice. Accept where we are right now. We are where we are because of the choices we have made. We signed all our own contracts. We created our life. If a correction is in order:

Own it, stop, and change now!

Knowing happens in the present moment. Let us claim our knowing. Embrace the inherent knowledge already within us. Let us integrate living our all-knowing into our life. Let us live as our original authentic true self. Remember, our **knowing is accessible to us right now and in every moment**. Decide to use it. When we are connected to God, we know. Know that we know!

> I do know. I trust myself.
> I trust my knowing. I am grateful for my knowing. I connect with the light of my knowing. I am aware and informed. I choose to live in the light of my knowing. I feel the light of my knowing. I use my knowing. I go forth with the knowing that everything I require is already in me. I know that God put all the answers already in me. I act on my knowing. I know what actions to take. Thank You God, for the clarity that comes with all-knowing.

Feel The Connection

Let us begin to always proceed from our knowing. Knowing is light and easy. Let us feel the presence of Christ in our life; feel the union and the oneness. Feel the love God has for us. Let us feel that **we are worthy**. Feel that we are a conduit in action for the Creator.

Part Two

Chapter 7

PRAYER
Talking to God

Let us be in communication with God through prayer. Prayer is speaking to God, and meditative contemplation is listening to Him. Prayer is an important part of establishing a relationship and sharing our heart with God. It is our individual petitioning, along with the opportunity to express gratitude to our Creator.

> "Do not be anxious about anything, but in every situation, by **prayer** and **petition,** with **thanksgiving, present your requests to God.**"
> —Philippians 4:6 (NIV)

Petitioning is a form of prayer with purpose. This way of prayer presents a formal request or asking, regarding a particular desire to God. I believe that this form of prayer was what God had in mind. He already knows our heart, yet listens for us to call forth our desires in His presence.

> ". . . concerning the work of My hands, **you command Me.**"
> —Isaiah 45:11 (NKJV)

Am I calling forth the work of His hands?

Prayer

How do I pray? I simply talk to God in casual, loving communication. I hold daily conversations with Him. I tell Him things like a close friend. I ask His advice. I ask for His blessing on my life every day. I ask Him to bless the people in my life and all humanity. I ask blessing on this whole world, and I declare His grace and His mercy to bless the Earth. He is always with me and I am in constant communication with Him. This is my fun.

I place myself completely in God's care. Thus, prayer creates an everlasting nearness to God. Let us visualize Him sitting with us. Talking to God strengthens our heart and transcends beyond our intellect.

After hurricane Irma, many screened pool enclosures were blown out, including ours. The availability of screen in our town was diminished, to a point that even the screen repair companies were waiting for material. Although my friend owns a screen company, we were 25th out of over 400 on his list.

After a few weeks of waiting, my husband reminded me that we were hosting a dinner party at our house and he planned to grill outside. The mosquitos, however, were plentiful. We had a second screen company come to the house that Monday to give us an estimate. I asked the guys where they normally purchase screen, and they told me the name of a hardware store in town. After inquiring, they also told me that the screen shipments come in on Tuesdays and Fridays. I replied, "Wonderful! Tomorrow is Tuesday and also my birthday, so I'll ask God to give me screen for my birthday." They laughed and said, "Good *luck*, lady!" I petitioned God and promised, "God, when You have this gift for me by Friday, I will be on my knees in praise and thanksgiving."

First thing the next day, I went to the hardware store and walked directly to the screen counter. They told me that they were out of screen and zero screen was expected. I found a lady who called to check for inventory at two other stores with the same result. However, she was kind enough to write up a purchase order for two rolls of 96" screen, because it was my birthday. She told me that if any screen comes in, she will have it delivered to this store. She also said that if they receive a delivery, she will call me and I can pay with my credit card over the phone. Before I left the store, I asked for the phone number of the manufacturer, and on my way home, I called the company to stay in my dream and grow my excitement about screen. The phone attendant explained to me the production procedure and how they had already increased to triple shifts and were delivering equally throughout the State, because everyone was asking for

Prayer

screen. They assured me they were doing everything possible to supply the demand.

Early Friday morning, the hardware store called, referencing an order and asking for my credit card number. At first, I was wondering what this was about, then all at once I remembered my birthday order! I paid and sent my daughter to the store. When she returned from the store, she had a fun story to tell: "When I went in the store and asked for my mom's screen, they looked at me as if I was out of this world and started laughing. However, my mom only sends me on errands with a reason, so I kindly asked them to look for the two rolls of screen I was to pick up with my mom's name on them. Just to humor me, they went to check. To their amazement, they came back with two rolls of screen with her name on it, and it was marked 'paid'. They were wondering how it got there. Was there a delivery? It was the weirdest look I saw on their faces."

When I asked my friend if he had time to install my screen, his first reaction was, "Which hardware store did you buy it at? I wish to buy screen for all my clients." I told him the name of the store and he called me back a few hours later to tell me, "I am at the store and they said that they are completely out of screen, and the last delivery they had was weeks ago! They denied ever having screen these past few

Connect To The Light

days. How did you obtain the screen?" My reply was, "I know the owner." **God owns it all!** I went on my knees in praise and thanksgiving, happily driving my screen around in victory with a big smile on my face for days, thanking God profoundly every time I looked at it.

Since my friend was still busy with other clients, I declared, "It is time to put up the screen on my lanai's cage." The second part of the order was the installation. I was also reminded that next time my asking can be more efficient; order the whole package at once: in this case, the screen plus the installation of it! I drove by the front gate of my community and asked for one of the men I knew working there to come by the house and install my screen. He came to the house the next morning. In 24 hours, everything was done.

Often, when we start ordering, we order one piece of the sandwich and the additional pieces as we move forward. We start with the bread and then add items we wish on it. Similarly, we are welcome to add unto our petitions or order the whole desired outcome at once.

Prayer can be expressed in many forms: speaking, writing, dancing, cheering, and singing praises to His holy name. Prayer is a privilege and an opportunity for us to personally communicate and stretch out our hands and our heart in whatever way we are comfortable, whatever action brings us the feeling of connection and joy. Let us sit down or stand up. Pray with our arms outstretched to heaven and our eyes focused on where our strength comes from, or bow down on our knees. Be in loving worship. Whatever type of prayer that focuses on God, and works for us, is welcomed by God. He loves our praises and thanksgiving. If we call on Him regularly, our connection muscle is built and we receive His guidance instantly. **Stay close to Him.**

Prayer is often thought of as a practice that is very formal, one that is defined by an organization. I like to put forth the inviting thought of prayer being a personal communication and a personal relationship with God. I am really speaking of a personal dance, a personal conversation, a personal way of reaching out and touching and feeling the connection between ourself and our divine Creator. This is how to have a personal walk, a friendship, with God. Welcome God's expertise into our life and ask for His help continually. Call upon Jesus, then simply trust Him, as He will take care of everything. We have a powerful friend and ally, a loving father and helpmate, an all-knowing, all-caring, and all-mighty king available to us. Let us embrace this privilege.

It is sort of doing away with the rules that so

many of us grew up with around prayer that it has to be done in a formal way, at a scheduled time, in a designated place, and repeated over and over. God hears us the first time and every time. Let us invite in new thought processes around the action of prayer.

We are all able to pray. **Pray often.** Let us pray as we wake up, over our meals, before we go to bed, and frequently throughout the day. Prayers are our intentions offered to and shared lovingly with God. As we are focusing on the positive, pray with a rejoicing heart full of thanksgiving. I think that, by opening our heart, we can incorporate a lot more intimacy into prayer. Let us seek Him first and continually with all our heart.

> "'For I know the plans I have for you,' declares the Lord, 'plans to prosper you and not to harm you, plans to give you hope and a future. Then you will **call on me** and come and **pray to me**, and **I will listen to you**. You will seek me and find me when you **seek me with all your heart.**'"
>
> —Jeremiah 29:11-13 (NIV)

Prayer

Pray into the solution. Let us pray with our eyes on the victory, while visualizing the achievement and enjoyment of our goals. Ask for the solution as if it is already granted. Use positive words and be in a positive mindset. The vibration of prayer is strong. Remember to pray that God's will and our will are aligned. Ask in victorious confidence.

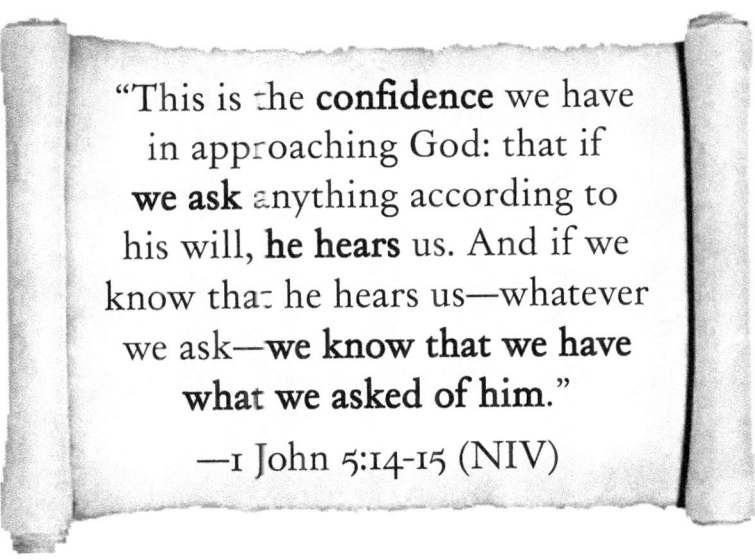

"This is the **confidence** we have in approaching God: that if **we ask** anything according to his will, **he hears** us. And if we know that he hears us—whatever we ask—**we know that we have what we asked of him.**"

—1 John 5:14-15 (NIV)

One day, when my daughter asked God for more time to study for her test, the professor cancelled it. My daughter and I talked about all the different occasions when God helped us through school. We both asked time after time, "Please God, help me to receive an A on the exam." In her case, the test is often cancelled or postponed and for me I just miraculously knew the answers. I recall one time, when the outcome of this prayer was hilarious. I handed in a long essay praying that I will receive the highest grade, thinking that if I had spent more time on it, I may have done better. When it was time to receive our grades, the teacher handed out all the students' papers except mine. Curious what grade I had, I asked the teacher. She turned red and answered, "You have the highest grade as usual." I inquired, "May I have my paper back?" She asked me to come see her after class, when she confessed to me that she was about to read my paper when her dog ate it. God answers in miraculous ways!

My daughters often pray over their tests and papers before they hand them in declaring that the teacher loves the answers and the assignments are done exactly the way the teacher desires. **Let us pray and speak the word over everything and be ready to smile, cheer, and praise when God delivers.**

How is our relationship with God? Let us create a direct, intimate relationship with our triune God: The Father, the Son, and the Holy Spirit. God gave us the Holy Spirit. He intercedes to the most high King for us on our behalf.

Prayer

> "In the same way, the Spirit helps us in our weakness. We do not know what we ought to pray for, but **the Spirit himself intercedes for us** through wordless groans. And he who searches our hearts knows the mind of the Spirit, because the Spirit intercedes for God's people in accordance with the will of God."
>
> —Romans 8:26-27 (NIV)

It is important for us to ask God through petitioning. The true joy is when we understand the power God wields. God is able to answer all prayer, because He created, and therefore has control over the entire Universe. He created the entire Universe and therefore has control over it. Everything is under His creation power and thus anything can be remolded and recreated at any time and all molecules can be moved in any way He desires. Everything can be affected by prayer, everything is God's turf. God can change everything, everywhere, anytime, in any given moment. God is in control all the time and He is in charge of our security. Call on Him. The more petitioning and asking that we do in prayer, the more wonder we can co-create with God.

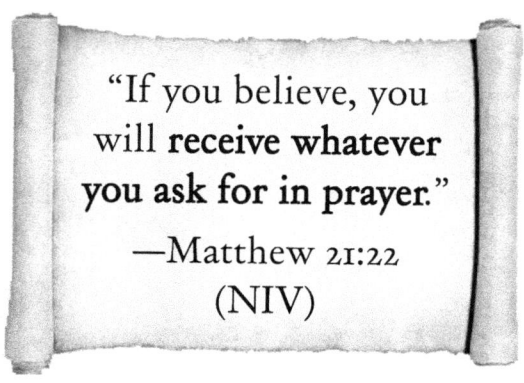

"If you believe, you will **receive whatever you ask for in prayer.**"
—Matthew 21:22
(NIV)

My sister recently shared her story of how her asking in prayer was answered very precisely:

With new cars we can now open our car doors with the key still in our purse or pocket. Given this, I find it more difficult to keep track of the two keys for my car. Previously, I misplaced my second car key and this type of key is very expensive to replace! Once again, I was searching for my spare key. This time, I knew it was somewhere in my home. I searched the house, the garage, my pockets, my husband's pockets, drawers, cabinets, everywhere. Then, over the course of more than one month,

Prayer

I searched a second and third time. It remained yet to be found. While searching, I decided to manifest having my key again.

Finally, I prayed, "God, Your Universe is powerful. I require my key right here, in my hand." I pointed to my palm. That same week I laid down on my Bemer mat, which I had been using every few days over the last month. When I laid down this time, the bed depressed with my weight on my right side and my lost key literally rolled right into the palm of my hand! I was amazed. I had to immediately give God the praise and glory; for His powerful Universe had very specifically placed the missing key "right here, in my hand" just as I asked.

When my children asked me if they may have my car and money late one Saturday night to buy chocolate, it sounded less than compelling to give them what they were asking for. Then I asked them **why** they had such a plan. "We wish to buy chocolate to make fresh chocolate chip cookies." As health is my joy, this reasoning was yet to be convincing. "Tomorrow is Father's Day. Dad loves homemade chocolate chip cookies. We are baking them for him as a gift to set out on the table when he comes for breakfast." Now that was compelling. Let us ask in detail, and also **include a compelling reason, in our**

prayers, petitions, and askings. Let us always be clear about **why** we love to have, do, and achieve everything.

Trust that God has our best interest at heart. Let us find a prayer partner who also has our best interest at heart. Use the Power of Agreement (see page 153). I desire for all of us to have a prayer partner: A person we share joy with, receive a second energy from, and are encouraged by.

I have prayer lists. One with all the names on it of people I know so that everyone is constantly prayed over. On another list, I have my current askings for today and a third list contains broader topics I wish to bring before God on a daily basis. This list includes askings I have for my family and friends as well as askings they have for themselves and requested me to pray for them.

In addition to declaring our goals, we can assist others with their desires. Let us pray for each other, loved ones, family, friends, doctors, government officials, leaders, pastors, churches, humanity, nations, happiness, harmony, health, and wealth; how about everything. God uses humanity to show His love. What a gift we can give to ourself and others any time, any place! It is free. Let us pray with sincere

Prayer

declaration, focused thought, loving words, and a pen to write everything down.

Create your prayer list. You may start one right in your journal and add to it continually.

Hold your prayer list and journals, containing the goals and desires for your life, in your hand, speak the words, and pray over the journals and your life.

"God, You know my heart. You know my goals and desires. Multiply my life, Lord. Bless me and favor me. Keep me inspired. You hold my askings. I receive my answered prayers. All is fulfilled. All is fulfilled. All is fulfilled. I praise You and I love You. Thank You. I am free."

Recently, I was in Ireland and I decided to go out and pray at a church. I walked around town for a while and stopped at the first church I passed. It was 5 p.m. There was an attendant at the door saying, "Sorry, the church is closing." I declared to him,

Connect To The Light

"I am here to pray. Is there a possibility for me to come in and pray?" He answered, "The father is doing the final prayer for the day. I have to lock the door. If you are okay being locked in the church for 20 minutes you may come in and pray. He will let you out when he is done with the closing prayer." I happily went in and prayed joy and God's light over the world as the father was reciting his written prayer. I was in exuberant joy and great satisfaction on the way home as this was my asking and God helped me to stay focused in prayer for 20 minutes.

Can we be in prayer and in the light for more than 20 minutes each day?

Pray the following prayer to connect to the light. Let us pray together!

Dear Father God,

You are the light of my life.
I am connected to You.

I welcome You into my heart and
I ask for Your guidance. Enlighten me.

Align my will with Your will and keep me
in Your righteous arena.

Prayer

I understand that my all-knowing
comes from You.

I listen to this higher knowing and I act on it.

Bless me and help me to keep my eyes
focused on You.

Stay with me all the days of my life.

I know I am worthy of Your love.

Remind me that I have enough courage.

Let me go forth in faith, confidence,
and praise.

Polish me so that my heart is like
a clear window so that Your light can shine
through me out into this world.

Let me be Your light to everyone
I see before me.

I am allowing Your light to show through me
into every possibility throughout my day.

God, You have blessed me.
Joy is mine forevermore.

I rejoice in You Jesus.

With Love, Gratitude, and Happiness,

Your loving Child

Connect To The Light

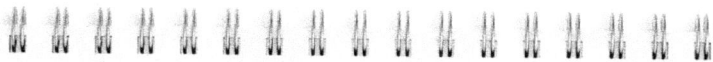

 Write your own prayer and have a continuous list of things you wish to bring before God and ask His help with.

Let us commune with the King of the Universe any time, any place. **Call on the name of Jesus. There is power in His name.** As we wish to become stronger spiritually, let us keep the name of Jesus on our lips and in our hearts.

> "And whatever you do, whether in word or deed, **do it all in the name of the Lord Jesus, giving thanks to God** the Father through him."
>
> —Colossians 3:17 (NIV)

Chapter 8

CONTEMPLATIVE MEDITATION
Listening To God

Meditation is the conscious practice of quieting the mind. It is a conscious exercise and starts with experiencing the presence of God. Being in contemplative meditation is to welcome in deep, reflective thoughts. It gives us an opportunity to:

- ♥ Experience God
- ♥ Spend quiet time alone with our inner self
- ♥ Center ourself, aligning our head with our heart
- ♥ Just breathe and recognize the power of our own breath
- ♥ Calm ourself and relax all our muscles
- ♥ Receive inspired thoughts and guidance

Connect To The Light

Let us find a place where we can relax and concentrate on ourself. We may choose a place inside or outside. It may be a favorite chair or a spot by the window where the sun is visible. We may enhance our meditation with essential oils or candles. We may also sit on a bench in a park or under a tree. Remember, our state of mind is more important than our surroundings. Quieting ourself can be done anywhere we are. It is a mindful choice to connect to our inner center.

To begin the practice of meditative contemplation, we may choose to sit with our hands relaxed on our lap and a straight spine or lie down comfortably.

Let us focus on our breath and consciously relax all our muscles. Focus on the sound of the inhalation and exhalation of the breath or a simple background sound such as calm music, the air conditioner, water dripping, or birds singing. To implement this practice into our daily life we may begin by using guided meditations.

We may meditate when we wake up in the morning to set our day in a relaxed, calm, peaceful, inspired state. A short meditation is also very effective to reset ourselves throughout the day when we require a moment to regroup, a change of mood, or enhanced energy. We may also use the time spent during

Contemplative Meditation

repetitive daily tasks such as taking a shower, folding the laundry, or washing the dishes as meditative experiences.

Let us have a quiet moment for ourself and listen. **Fifteen to twenty minutes daily** is proven to be most effective. Let us consciously choose to take time and just be.

We have two ears and one mouth. Thus, we shall listen twice as much as we speak. Let us be quiet with ourself in contemplation and listen to God. Let us be part of a two-way communication with Him. We voiced our prayers, now let us hear His plans for us. Let us align our will with His perfect will as we receive inspired messages. Let us hear His voice and welcome His guidance.

> Dear God, as I calm myself into this meditative state for 15 minutes, I am welcoming in all guidance that comes from You. I am wide open. I am free to receive. Show me Your will. Thank you.

Connect To The Light

One lady who is leading a large corporation told me once that she walks every morning. During this walk she clears her mind completely and she asks God to show her what His will is for this day. After she returns from her walk, she plans her day incorporating all the insight she received on her morning walk.

Let us be encouraged to take a few moments every day to close our eyes, to follow our breath, to go within and look inside our heart, to calm down and to be still. Let us remove everything from our conscious mind. This way we are able to look at all new thoughts coming in and allow them to flow through us. When we allow ourself to be in a meditative state for a few minutes, ideas will enter our mind. These ideas are our meditative inspirations. When we are calm and relaxed, let us be conscious and honor the **first thought** we receive in this state. The first thought our subconscious sends us is our inspired thought. Meditative contemplation is more than clearing our mind of all thought, it is about **allowing great leads to come in**. These messages are such an important piece of our connection and creation power.

Contemplative Meditation

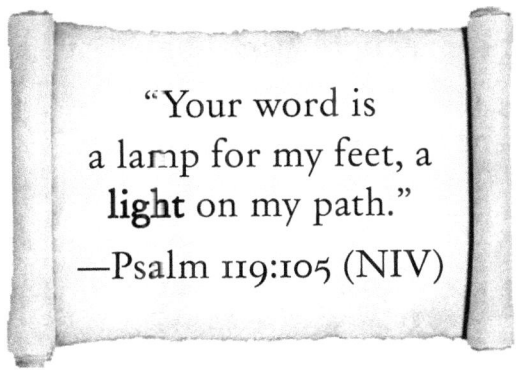

"Your word is a lamp for my feet, a **light** on my path."
—Psalm 119:105 (NIV)

Let us make sure to write down all inspired thoughts immediately after our contemplation time. Note all people, places, things, and ideas that popped into our head. Because we record these messages, we can act on our first ideas when we are ready. Great things happen when we **act on our inspired thoughts**.

We may experience that a certain person or a certain place from our past pops into our conscious awareness. Let us make sure we send a positive thought and light to this person or place. It may be time to re-connect. We can pray over them or call them.

One Friday evening I was sitting in class. My stomach started to make itself known and my thoughts drifted to dinner options. I began contemplating which dish will satisfy me. The Pei Wei restaurant popped into my head. I knew I was passing right by it on the way home. I was silently asking for the teacher to finish early so that the restaurant was still open. Now, I was absolutely looking forward to my Pei Wei dinner. I did make it shortly before closing and the joy of dinner and a movie at home was flowing through me. When I came home, I grabbed my apple juice from the refrigerator and found another Pei Wei dish inside with the lovely note, "For whoever is hungry for Pei Wei, feel free to eat." Wow, God had covered my Pei Wei dinner in advance. In contemplation, I sent out my thoughts with the mission to receive my favored dinner.

A friend of mine shared this beautiful story with me: I was driving down the road and I was imagining and embracing radiant health. I had a passing thought that maybe it will be good to cleanse my liver. That night on my doorstep was a heavy brown package, and I wondered what it might be. When I opened the package, it was a book called *Liver Rescue*.

My name was on the label, yet did I order it? It turned out that my brother ordered it for me, as he too is interested in health.

Contemplative Meditation

The minute the thought transmits out to the whole Universe, it transforms instantly. All the pieces are floating and waiting to be ordered with love.

This is a great example of the illusion of time. If we think about time linearly, the agreement over the initial thought occurred after the book was ordered and sent. However, the book was placed on the doorstep by the delivery man immediately after the thought. This is why some scientists believe that we are moving backwards in "time," so that everything can coordinate in the right moment.

All answers and solutions already exist. Inspired thoughts from our meditation or contemplation really matter, because we are tapping into this all-knowing. We are all connected through a universal web and when we allow ourself to play in this energy field, connection just happens automatically. Being in a meditative state is like entering into the throne room with God, being in His presence and experiencing His rest as we are strengthening our connection to the light.

Allow whatever floats in to float in. We may also be very accurate and focus on any situation or topic. The Five Minute Couch Time introduced in chapter three (page 53) is also a very helpful contemplation exercise. It entails entering into meditation with a question in mind. For example, we may meditate about our perfect health, relationships, wealth, or on God's Word.

"I will meditate on
your precepts
and fix my eyes on
your ways."
—Psalm 119:15 (NIV)

Receive Joy offers a guided *Connect To The Light Mediation* using only positive words. It is designed to help us relax and connect to the light. For convenience and delight, this Receive Joy meditation is available on CD or to download at www.receivejoy.com. Please listen to it as often as desired to have uplifting thoughts, to feel good, and practice connection. Let us clear our minds and open our awareness for our cup of life to continuously refill and runneth over.

Contemplative Meditation

> "May these words of my mouth and this meditation of my heart be pleasing in your sight, LORD, my Rock and my Redeemer."
> —Psalm 19:14 (NIV)

Let us sit quietly and listen through the heart.

Chapter 9

READ THE HOLY BIBLE

God left us *The Holy Bible*; His inspired Word recorded through men's hands. The Bible is our manual to this life experience. It is the greatest love story ever written to us, His children. Through His stories, teachings, advice, and words God shows His love for humanity.

Every year, the Bible is the number one best-selling book in the world. It supersedes all other book sales by such a great margin because humankind's powerful and universal desire to know God and His Word is continual. This means that people find great value in this book. **The Bible continues to steer us and solidifies our connection to Him.**

Reading the Bible leads us to a deeper spiritual

Read The Holy Bible

relationship with our Creator. **The more often we read the Bible and meditate on it, the more we will absorb divine inspiration.** His Living Word helps us to gain a fuller understanding of God and His eternal plan.

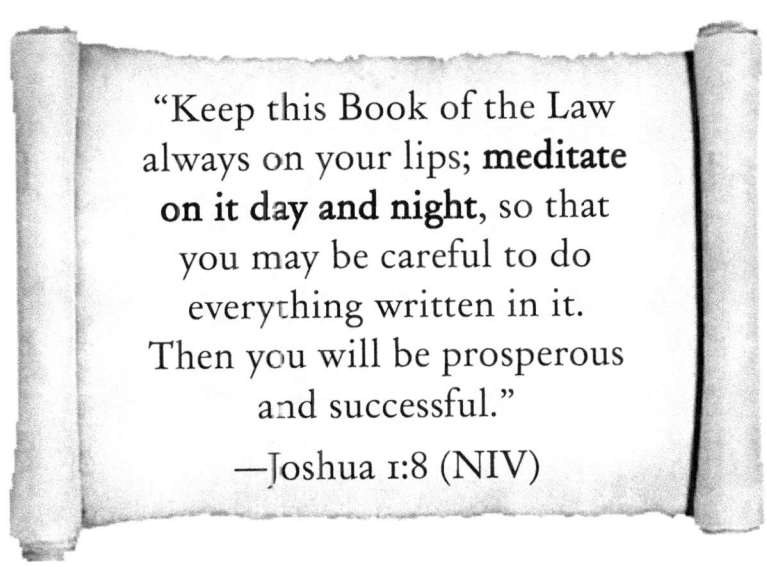

"Keep this Book of the Law always on your lips; **meditate on it day and night**, so that you may be careful to do everything written in it. Then you will be prosperous and successful."
—Joshua 1:8 (NIV)

The Bible is the one book that contains God's wisdom. Wise men still seek Him, His wisdom, and His teachings. The Bible is full of simple, beautiful advice on how to live a healthy, happy, awesome life. The Holy Bible is a book that teaches us about personal well-being, our relationship with this world and the absolutes of the Universe.

Reading it every day, meditating on the Word, and

Connect To The Light

speaking it out keeps us connected to God's light. His Word fills us up and keeps us coming back for more.

Pick up your Bible, open it, and read it daily. For a beautiful start of your day, Receive Joy suggests reading the Bible 15 minutes every morning.

Read it out loud.

Pick a verse and take it to heart and contemplate it.

Memorize one verse a day.

Write the verse in your journal in your own handwriting.

How does the Bible verse relate to you today? Journal your thoughts as well.

Read The Holy Bible

OWN A BIBLE

If you happen to require a Bible, go and obtain one; or more than one! Own your personal Bible! Yes, you can download an app; however, there is something magical in seeing and feeling God's inspired Word printed on paper.

Thrift stores sell used Bibles for a small price. Every bookstore and online bookseller carries this bestseller.

There are different versions you can choose from. Some have Jesus' Words highlighted in red, others are color-coded by topic.

The Bible comes in different translations. If you are purchasing a Bible for the first time, you may wish to pick a translation that is easy to read. In that case, you may choose the New Living Translation (NLT). The version thought by some to be most accurately translated is the New American Standard Bible (NASB). Bible studies commonly choose the New International Version (NIV). The New King James Version (NKJV) is widely favored. There are many other versions. Select one that you are drawn to.

STUDY YOUR BIBLE

Use your Bible actively—every day of the week. Highlight passages, underline verses, take notes on the pages, post sticky notes. Be familiar with your Bible. Allow it to be a best friend that offers the best advice. Let it talk to you. Let the Living Word inspire you. Gain intimacy with the best book ever written!

Receive Joy suggests reading with the books of Ephesians and Galatians. The Apostle Paul wrote these books as encouragement to the followers of Christ through his voice.

Some people make it a habit to read the Bible every year from beginning to end. Some follow a reading plan. You can find reading plans online, at Christian bookstores, in churches, or in apps. Many churches and communities offer Bible studies for different topics throughout the year in small groups. There are also plenty of online classes from which to choose. If you are experiencing a certain circumstance in your life right now that requires uplifting, customized classes are offered for everything; for example, single parenting, loss of a loved one, increasing your faith, and much more.

Read The Holy Bible

When I spent a semester studying at a Christian college, I barely knew Christ and my first Bible was fresh. For all my assignments, I was asked to include Bible verses. My first question as a Business Psychologist was, are my study topics covered in this book? Are there verses for the classes I am taking; what can the Bible tell me about "Counseling Therapies," "Motivation," "Gender, Self, and Society," "Public Relations," and "Entrepreneurship?" After days picking through the pages asking God to guide me to matching verses to complete my course assignments, He led me to discover that my Bible had a reference list in the back with all kinds of topics. What a joy!

Years later, I learned that I can put the topic I am looking for in a search engine online in connection with "Bible verse" and matching verses pop up. On one hand, I am happy that I was encouraged to take a physical Bible in my hand, page through it, and become familiar with it. On the other hand, the online search is a real time saver.

> "All Scripture is God-breathed and is useful for teaching, rebuking, correcting and training in righteousness, so that the servant of God may **be thoroughly equipped for every good work.**"
>
> —II Timothy 3:16-17 (NIV)

The scriptures in the Bible are God-breathed, inspired by God himself. It is the Living Word. Every time we pick up the Bible there is a new inspiration, a new idea, and another layer to discover. Ivan Panin spent over 50 years of his life exploring the supernatural numeric structure of scripture as proof of its divine inspiration.

It all comes down to one simple action: **Let us open our Bible and start reading daily.** Seek out the truth of God's Word to help us Connect First, Connect to the Light, to Feel the Connection and to stay in His light. **Live in the light of God's Word.** Let Him speak to you. Be encouraged to pick up the

Read The Holy Bible

Holy Bible and begin to know it intimately! Let us imprint His Word in our hearts. In the words of King David:

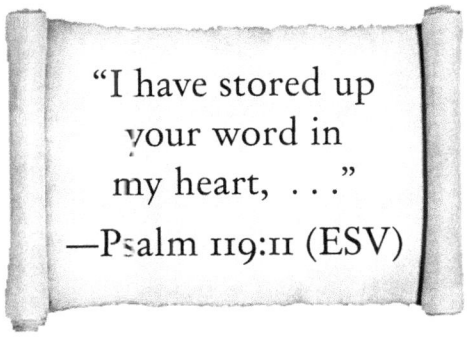

"I have stored up
your word in
my heart, . . ."
—Psalm 119:11 (ESV)

Chapter 10

COMMUNITY

God wishes for us to be in community. Humans are made for relationships and unity. Joyful social interactions with friends and family are true blessings. Throughout the Bible, there are many accounts where community was essential. Noah took His family on the Ark. Moses led the Jewish nation out of Egypt and toward the Promised Land. Jesus chose twelve disciples. God has twenty-four elders assembled around His throne twenty-four hours a day worshipping Him who lives for ever and ever (Revelation 4:4,10).

There are many ways we can be in community:

- ♥ Have and maintain significant relationships with family and friends

Community

- ♥ Have a best friend
- ♥ Have a prayer partner or accountability partner you meet with regularly
- ♥ Have a business partner
- ♥ Attend church, prayer groups, or Bible Study
- ♥ Join or create a Miracle Group
- ♥ Have a mentor or coach
- ♥ Join a Master Mind group
- ♥ Surround yourself with five people that have talents you wish to acquire
- ♥ Join a club
- ♥ Join Receive Joy's network: Million True Millionaires (www.milliontruemillionaires.com)
- ♥ Volunteer with a charity
- ♥ Attend seminars
- ♥ Attend or participate in sporting events
- ♥ Pour love into your children and grandchildren
- ♥ Befriend a neighbor

Connect To The Light

- ♥ Befriend a younger person
- ♥ Befriend an older person
- ♥ Smile and wave at everyone
- ♥ Share the love of this beautiful Universe

Let us spend more quality time with loved ones. Let us make sure that all the relationships we regularly maintain are encouraging and uplifting. Let us share joy. Call friends and neighbors together to relax, have fellowship with, and rejoice.

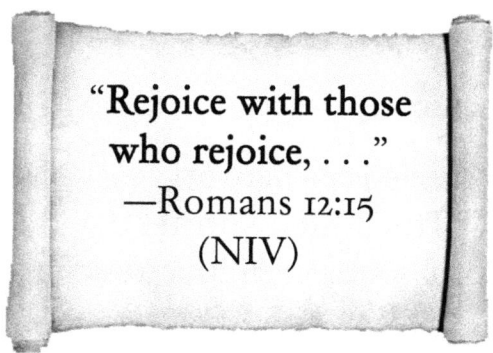

"Rejoice with those who rejoice, . . ."
—Romans 12:15
(NIV)

God set up **a powerful mechanism** in the Universe that honors and carries out the **agreement between two or more parties**:

Community

> "Again I say to you, if **two** of you **agree** on earth about anything they ask, it will be done for them by my Father in heaven. For where two or three gather in my name, there am I with them."
> —Matthew 18:19-20 (NIV)

This **Power of Agreement** is similar to a 1.5-volt battery combined with another 1.5-volt battery. When they are linked together, they become more powerful than the individual alone. When a flashlight requires two batteries, the light only turns on when both are in place. We are multipliers. God set up the Universe in a way that when two or more individuals come together, the light begins to shine even brighter and miracles happen.

This is how board meetings of large companies are run to set their goals. One person introduces an idea or a motion and another member of the board seconds the motion. The administrative assistant writes it down and the motion is passed.

Similarly, we have this ability to create with the agreeing force of another individual. The other person can participate in agreement and encouragement of our set goals even when the other person is only slightly aware of the content. We can "high five" each other or have the other person initial our written statement, speak about it, or partake in whatever method with which we feel comfortable.

Whether people go to seminars, concerts, live sporting events, or gather in church and pray on Sundays, they are all sharing the elevated vibrational energy of the group. When we **pray in a group**, we enhance our focus and desires. This is why Jesus gathered His disciples and sent them out two at a time. Let us gather in brotherhood like in the days of Jesus and pray, worship, and praise Him in community.

Let us find a friend that is our second energy, our prayer partner, and our accountability partner to lift our spirit and vibration. Moses was only able to hold his arms high with the staff given by the Lord to achieve victory because he had Aaron and Hur assisting him. Let us hold each other lifted up.

Community

> *Have a prayer or accountability partner with whom you pray regularly and share each other's goals and askings. Talk about your gains achieved and miracles created.*

In 2013, a group of friends decided to come together regularly and practice positive intentions. The reason for the meetings is to focus on the good in every moment and experience the Power of Intentional Asking. During our meetings, we share positive words and energy; we learn, listen, and refine our manifesting skills. We are likeminded individuals who help and encourage each other and have open-minded conversations. We share our desires and what we are asking to receive. We write down our goals and desires in our journals and second each other's askings. Then, in the following meetings, we share in the joy of each other's empowering creation stories and the goals we achieved, all the while encouraging each other with great love and gratitude. We practice collective intention-setting with other likeminded positive people using the Power of Agreement.

We meet every two weeks for most of the year. These meetings have become a place for meaningful friendships, support, inspirations, respect, love, acceptance of all, reminders, joy, and rediscovering the truth. This is our **Miracle Group**. We embrace with optimism that we are part of the Oneness of Humanity.

Join a Miracle Group meeting or start your own Mastermind Group.

It is said that we become like the five people we surround ourself with most. Thus, choose these people deliberately. Let us surround ourself with five people or more that have mastered values and skills that we wish to grow into. We may have a group of five experts for different areas of our life. Consider hiring **a trained professional**; a tutor, mentor, or coach. These highly trained and knowledgeable individuals are successful in their respective fields and help us grow and expand our vision.

Community

To ensure that everyone has a community of all positive, encouraging people, we founded Million True Millionaires (MTM). MTM is an opportunity to connect with like-minded, purpose-driven individuals who strive for growth, contribution, and love. Let us all use this platform to share our visions, prayers, and askings, and receive seconding energies. All our members are constantly prayed over. Browse the free growth content in the library. Let us all share our products and services. This social network will help us find new business partners and friends. Our purpose is for all members of the MTM community to succeed together, as we encourage each other along the way. Let us all grow abundantly together in happiness, health, and wealth.

Be in community!

Come join us at

www.milliontruemillionaires.com

Chapter 11

FLOW WITH NATURE

God is expressing Himself through humanity and nature. Nature is perfect. God created everything in perfection. There is an innate understanding in nature. Nature obeys God's laws. Nature flows and continues on. Nature follows God's seasons. We also flow and transition with the seasons. The Earth rotates around the sun and we are privileged to experience the sensation of sunrises and sunsets. Most of nature comes alive when the sun is visible and rests as darkness appears.

Flow With Nature

> *On a sunny day, take 10 minutes and sit in the sunlight. What do you feel? Write down what you feel:*
>
> _____
> _____
> _____
> _____
> _____

In the sunlight, I feel: Warm, happy, relaxed, quiet, at peace, energized, activated, calm, soothed, good, reassured, and connected. Feel the incredible surge of energy we receive from the rays of the sun.

Sitting in the sun made me realize another duality of light: the calming, relaxing, quiet aspect of it in addition to the energizing, activating part. My mood lifted instantly to joyous and happy. I felt en**light**enment. My body was "charging." As solar panels harnessing light energy, we too receive nourishment from sitting in the sun, being with ourself and our Creator, while welcoming a recharge of our batteries.

> Go outside and experience nature.
>
> Be outside, take a walk, let the sun shine on your face, feel the wind on your skin, sit by a stream, feel the power of a waterfall or the soothing rhythm of waves. Feel the grass between your toes, enjoy gardening, take a hike, go swimming, enjoy outdoor life, smell the roses, experience nature's profound silence, hug a tree. See the beauty everywhere.

When I went to a camp in the Blue Ridge Mountains, I took a hike to a magnificent old oak tree. To surround the trunk, it took 12 adults. After everyone left, I sat in silent contemplation and felt the tree calling to me. I had the urge to hug it and place my head on its bark. I felt a wave of calmness come over me. I felt oneness. My frequency adjusted to the tree's frequency.

Like most of us, I also enjoy watching animals.

Flow With Nature

I have two small turtles swimming in my pool. The lessons I learn from them are treasures: Sit in silence, sit in the sun, and let the sun shine on you. Floating in the pool can be done all day long and God still takes good care of me with His provisions. Play with a friend.

We are the only ones being distracted as our mind and our thoughts wander to the past and to the future. Animals just live in the moment, while we often live in yesterday, rethinking yesterday's thoughts and contemplating what-ifs and what might have been. We can learn from nature.

Let us be in the present moment and experience nature's rhythm. Nature behaves according to God's plan. We notice that nature rhythmically flows according to God's plan. We humans tend to devise and follow our own plans separated from God. We are where we are and what we are because of our thoughts, words, and deeds. We are compelled to react to things that come by catching our attention. We swim against the current and use so much extra energy. Oftentimes, we push against the flow when we seek the feeling of being in control. Since we are a higher form of intelligence, let us learn to flow with God's plan and choose to be happy. Let us acknowledge that God's perfect plan is already in place.

When we look at the night sky, we notice that

the stars are in constant movement. They travel in a hypnotic rhythm. God set up the Universe containing this special rhythm of flow and allow. We are put on this Earth to flow with that same powerful movement. All vibrations we send out are returned to us. The same hypnotic rhythm binds our dominant thoughts and all our thought patterns. Our upbringing and family values also have influence on our thoughts. We reap what we sow. Permanent opulent thoughts of goodness and abundance create flow. Thus, all our thoughts, words, and deeds spin a three-dimensional web. This web holds us and either builds us up and lifts us above worldly influence or binds us fast to it.

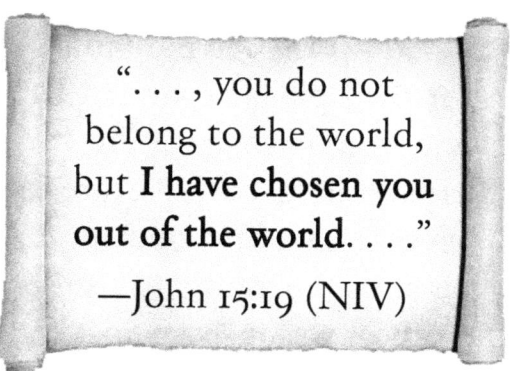

" . . . , you do not belong to the world, but **I have chosen you out of the world.** . . . "
—John 15:19 (NIV)

It is our conscious choice to spin our web and actively design our life in goodness. Let us fill it with the light of God. Thus, we are in this world and yet

Flow With Nature

lifted up to God's world through our connection to Him. The law of hypnotic rhythm is available to all. Use it in uplifting ways! Positive thinking, positive speaking, and good deeds are pleasing to ourself and God. Let us continually practice our connection to God.

All living beings change. Change is natural; we grow, we expand, we transform. We all know the story of the butterfly that has to break out of its cocoon to develop the strength in its wings to fly. Let us desire and embrace change. Change holds promise. Life is about progress, transformation, and moving forward while experiencing joy. Let us respond in joyful ways to change. We change in every moment. Our physical body renews itself completely every seven to ten years. God has made us that special.

As we **choose to embrace change**, we may ask, "Can one human being influence and change many things?" The answer is a definite yes. Throughout history, we have numerous examples of one human being having a vision, focusing on it, and having the courage to embrace that change. When they completely surrendered to their desired outcome in a peaceful and positive way, all change began. Positive examples are: Mahatma Gandhi, Nelson Mandela, Mother Teresa, Reinhard Bonnke, Nicola Tesla,

Connect To The Light

Thomas Edison, Henry Ford, Bill Gates, and Steve Jobs.

To change anything, let us first change our mind. The mind is a powerful creator; so powerful that it is the source that convinces us to do everything. Before any change is possible, we shall consciously welcome in the opportunity to improve our thought processes. **Let us focus on the good in every moment.** Change starts with our mind. Change happens when we focus our awareness on what we truly desire and target what brings us the most joy. We achieve this through our thoughts, speech, and writing.

Let us step out from our own shadow, surrender, and connect to God's light. Rejoice in His creation and flow with the natural rhythm God designed and desires for us.

Chapter 12

RECEIVE JOY

When I went around the world and handed out my Receive Joy business card to people I met, I often heard the comment, "I can use some more joy." **We all can use more joy in our life.**

Are we rejoicing? Can we live the rest of our life in joy? We shall do everything in happy celebration. We shall be enjoying every moment and every breath of our life. Life is fun! Focus on all the joy we can have. It is one thing to move through life achieving wonderful things, yet it takes a committed decision to **joyfully** achieve wonderful things.

Let us ponder if our life's success up to this point has been full of joy. From this point on, let us consciously decide to succeed with joy. **Do everything with joy.**

Let us travel our path in pure joy. Realize it is our choice to have happiness and joy in every moment, because this life is our experience. Choose to receive joy. Let us rejoice always!

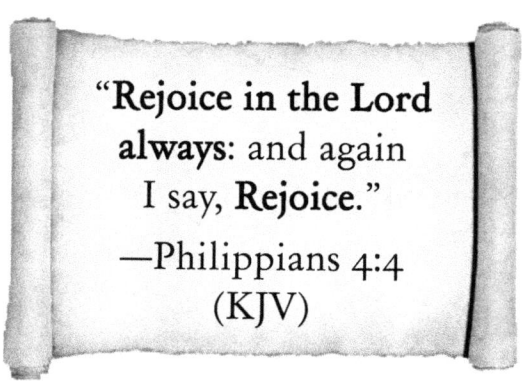

"Rejoice in the Lord **always**: and again I say, **Rejoice**."
—Philippians 4:4 (KJV)

A while back, when I was beginning to be consciously aware of the power of words, I realized that a friend of mine has joy in his last name. He was very happy to discuss this fact, and he tells everyone he meets about it, thus declaring it over and over. Now, whenever he is in a mood less than joy, he reminds himself to return back into a joyful state immediately to honor his name.

How can we be more joyful? First, practice being happy. Let us **decide to be happy: Smile, laugh, be cheerful, be helpful**. Let us cheer ourself on by talking to ourself with encouraging words such as,

Receive Joy

> *I am happy and
> well all the time.
> I am joyful.
> Life is good.
> I smile all the time.
> I am a joyful soul.
> I view my world friendly.*

In this way, we are a blessing in everyone's life, and in turn, allow others to bless us.

Let us pick up and hold onto the joy in our own life. Joy is always here. It is a stand-alone. It lies like a coin on our table. Let us pick it up, put it in our pocket, and **take joy with us everywhere we go**.

Joy is one of the highest emotional vibrations. Let us check on what is happening with us vibrationally. Are we ready to vibrate in joy and stay here? To achieve anything, we shall first become its vibrational match. To be in the vibration of joy, we have to choose to be joyful. Conscious thought and pure desire set us up to be in a joyful receiving mode. Simply choose to align with happiness. Let us have all our actions be influenced by love and joy. Let us find our inner joy and live here. When we are filled up with joy, joy can radiate from us. As we vibrate in joy, we attract more joy. God desires us to rejoice.

Staying in joy is our first victory. Every thought attracts on a vibrational level. **Every positive thought attracts positive results into our reality.**

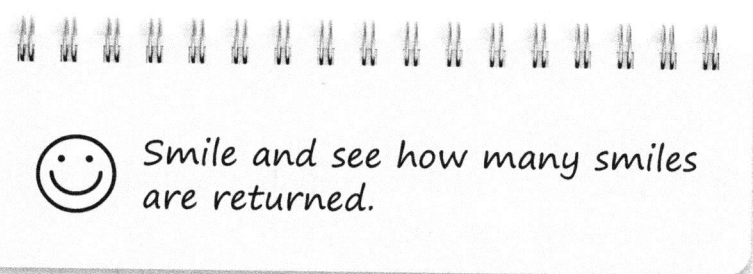

Smile and see how many smiles are returned.

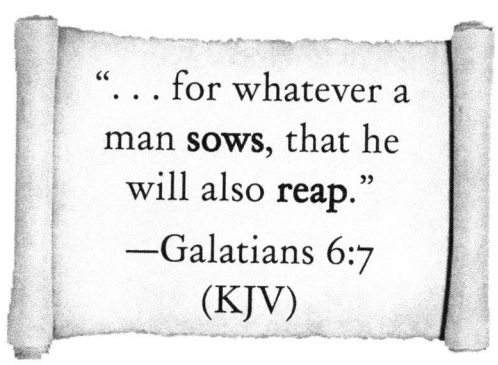

"... for whatever a man **sows**, that he will also **reap**."
—Galatians 6:7
(KJV)

Receive Joy

Every thought we think returns to us in physical manifestation. Our life mirrors our thoughts. As we choose our thoughts, we create our life and our world. Let us live our happy, joyful life by design. **Every thought affects our health and happiness.** Every thought we think is important!

I love asking big, and I receive my inspirations from all around me. One of my brother's askings is to be a treasure finder, and I really love the idea of being a treasure finder myself. I wrote in my *Daily Asking Journal* that I will find treasures—gold, silver, and jewels. So far, I usually find treasures in thrift stores, so I am continually on the look-out. I said, "I am open for everything, God. You can bring me treasures all the time." The next morning, my mother and I went for a walk on the beach. I played around with my feet in the sand by the edge of the water, when suddenly something was dancing around my toes. Earlier that morning I was admiring an orange inchworm on a beautiful orange flower in my kitchen window, and thanked God for all the beautiful creatures He created; all in a very unique and fun way. As the thing by my feet was dancing the same way the inchworm moved, I thought it to be another animal. Looking closer, I picked it up and it turned out to be a shiny emerald bracelet. I found my first treasure! God is so fun and creative in presenting us with what we ask for. Like attracts like: An orange inchworm on an orange flower and the emerald bracelet was found in the green-blue waters of Emerald Isle. God talks about the emerald light around His throne in Revelation, and now, when I wear my bracelet, I think of His emerald light.

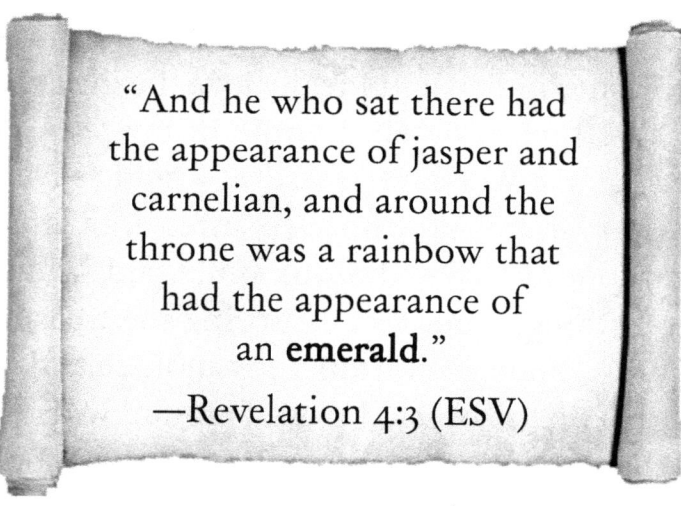

"And he who sat there had the appearance of jasper and carnelian, and around the throne was a rainbow that had the appearance of an **emerald**."
—Revelation 4:3 (ESV)

Let us also start declaring our joy out loud. We can use the following affirmations as a daily reminder that joyful solutions are available in every moment.

Receive Joy

> My life is full of joy.
> Every day I wake up
> I am so grateful.
> I have God's powerful Spirit within me.
> My joy aligns me with God.
> I embrace all the wonder
> the Universe has to offer.
> All goodness and wonder flow into my
> life continuously.
> Everything is always turning out
> in my favor.
> All is well all the time.

As we allow joy to pour into our cup, our self-love and self-confidence increase. Joy has renewal forces. Joy gives us the vitality and initiative to fulfill our desires and ambitions. **When we remain in joy, we are powerfully connected to the light.**

Chapter 13

CONTRIBUTION

Humans strive to belong to a community and share love. Our true potential can be met through one powerful action: Contribution. Some of the many ways we can contribute are through:

- ♥ Our service
- ♥ Our time
- ♥ Our knowledge
- ♥ Our talents
- ♥ Our prayer and petitioning on someone's behalf
- ♥ Our encouraging and seconding energy
- ♥ Physical blessings such as money and material donations

Contribution

When a friend asked to borrow money, I prayed and asked God to provide the finances if He wished for me to give the loan. The next day, I went to Freshman Orientation with my youngest daughter. Throughout the day, we received many miraculous offers that saved a lot of money. To my great joy, I found out our county is paying for two years of my daughter's college books. Opening a new student bank account came with a special introductory offer that included $200 and a free T-shirt. These savings and offers kept on coming even the next day, starting with a free investment in bitcoin for the same amount as the loan. I received more than I asked for, and through this, God demonstrated His provision to me, and I wrote the check to my friend the same day. **God's grace abounds.**

> "Every man shall **give** as he is able, **according to the blessing of the LORD** your God which He has given you."
>
> —Deuteronomy 16:17
> (NASB)

Contribution is sharing forth what God has given us. All gifts are from Him, including our talents, all that we own, and our finances. **Let us contribute to this beautiful world with our gifts, ideas, and energy.** Let us create something great. Let us call our life-long dreams into existence. Let us always be engaged in projects we are excited about and make our heart sing. Let us also be involved in a cause that helps the greater good.

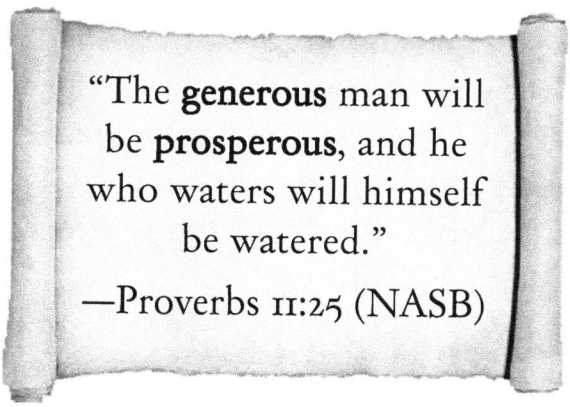

"The **generous** man will be **prosperous**, and he who waters will himself be watered."
—Proverbs 11:25 (NASB)

As part of educating my children in financial freedom and to be aware of the cost of goods they wish to have, I gave them each $1,000 in $100 bills. I also wished for them to see how long this amount will last. Out of this money they were to pay for everything themselves: Clothes, movie tickets and

Contribution

popcorn, toys, treats, etc. It was fun to see the choices they made.

My youngest daughter was five years old at that time, and shortly after I gave her the cash, she appeared back in the living room waving the first fresh $100 bill, asking us, "Do you know what I will do with this money?" She promptly answered, "I am putting this money in my purse to give to church on Sunday." I was happily surprised. All the Sundays she attended church, she already mastered the concept of giving her first ten percent.

I knew she was a cheerful giver from a very young age. When she was four, we went on a cruise and stopped in Mexico. She saw an elderly man selling necklaces on the sidewalk. She walked over to the nearest bench, emptied her little purse filled with change and a couple crumpled dollar bills, and gave him everything. She also declared, "Tomorrow, I will come back and give him the rest of the money I have, so that he can buy himself a store to sell his necklaces in."

Connect To The Light

Please ask yourself:
What can I contribute?

_____
_____
_____
_____
_____

What are my talents?

_____
_____
_____
_____
_____

Contribution

What can I spend hours on and it seems like seconds?

_____
_____
_____
_____

What am I excited about?

_____
_____
_____
_____
_____

Connect To The Light

What makes my heart leap with joy?

_____
_____
_____
_____

What can I contribute right now?

_____
_____
_____
_____

Contribution

Take the last idea you just wrote down and do it right now!

Here are some ideas:

- ♥ Share positive encouraging words
- ♥ Spread your positivity and kindness through smiles and hugs
- ♥ Cheer your friends on in the projects about which they are excited
- ♥ Share your abundance with others: give your extra clothes and household items that are just sitting in your house to a good cause
- ♥ Help a friend—ask what they require help with: organizing, babysitting, or running errands
- ♥ Call someone to wish them a happy new day
- ♥ Invite someone out for lunch or buy some groceries for someone you know who can appreciate this gift

Connect To The Light

- ♥ Do small daily acts of kindness
- ♥ Mentor a younger person in your trade or profession
- ♥ Volunteer
- ♥ Help children and the elderly
- ♥ Sponsor a child in your community or through a charity such as World Vision or Compassion International
- ♥ Pick two charities you are excited about and give them time and money

We are the creators, inviters, and attractors of all things in our life. Share the bounty God has already bestowed on us. Every good that goes out of us comes right back, as does everything else. Let us choose to radiate what is good, kind, blessed, loving, encouraging, and uplifting. God always provides us with many seeds for us to sow. Let us use our seeds generously. Everything belongs to God.

Contribution

> "Remember this: Whoever sows sparingly will also reap sparingly, and **whoever sows generously will also reap generously**. Each of you should **give** what you have decided in your heart to give, not reluctantly or under compulsion, for **God loves a cheerful giver**. And God is able to make all grace abound to you, so that always having all sufficiency in everything, you may have an abundance for every good deed."
>
> —II Corinthians 9:6-8 (NIV)

God loves a cheerful giver. God loves when we show appreciation for humanity by sharing with and taking care of our brothers and sisters in Christ. Let us give cheerfully from our heart and know that what we sow comes back to us. The biggest contribution we can give to ourself and others is love.

Connect To The Light

"A new command I give you: **Love one another.** As I have loved you, so you must love one another."

—John 13:34 (NIV)

Chapter 14

JOURNALING

Let us start to live by design and script our own story. Make journaling a priority. Journaling enhances our conscious creation power and helps us to focus on what we wish to call in. In order to advance our life, let us write into the solution. Journaling, asking, and editing are part of creating a focused productive life by design. As we are writing, remember that our beautiful words create our beautiful life.

First, we journal our gratitude, then our goals and askings, and further we keep track by journaling our gains: Our goals reached, blessings received, and desires met. Whenever we have received answers to our askings and prayers, we write them down to have a fantastic record of all we have gained and the miracles we have witnessed. Let us pick up our old journals regularly and be joyful about our gains.

This helps us build our confidence and develops our creation muscle.

Let us use time in the evening before we go to bed to review our day and recall everything we did, opportunities we received, and the people we met who brought us closer to our goals. This time of reflection serves to show us that we are responsible for our choices, our creations, and our growth.

Let us write down our words to bring them into this physical dimension, giving form to our creation. When we write our words on paper, we can change and add to them. There is great power in the pen. Let us read over our journaled words and edit our words three times. As pointed out in the chapter "The Power of Using Positive Words" in *Ask And You Shall Receive*, let us make sure that:

- ♥ Everything is stated in the positive
- ♥ Our words are uplifting and a blessing
- ♥ Our focus is clear and determined
- ♥ Everything is written in the present tense as if it is happening or has already happened and is here now
- ♥ Articulate why we desire to receive our askings

Journaling

Let us connect to the light by organizing our thoughts, setting clear intentions through written askings, speaking them out loud, praying over them, and staying open to receive with gratitude and confidence.

One time during our Miracle Group meeting I asked the members to share with me their journaling experiences. One member shared that she asked for a loving experience with an animal. Two days later, in a grocery store, she had a loving encounter with a Golden Labrador, and she enjoyed the love pouring from the animal while petting him. Now she can record this in the "gains and miracles" section of her journal and be grateful for this blessing bestowed unto her.

The same member shared that sometimes she is reluctant to write in her journal daily, and instead she refrains from doing so. I was surprised about her response, because I knew that everything she asked

Connect To The Light

for came into existence. Her answer was, "Exactly! Everything I write down comes to be. To celebrate my creations to the fullest and enjoy all the miracles flowing into my life, I choose to be selective with my journaling." This is the overflowing abundance God promises!

When we journal daily and make our goals and askings known, we are able to keep record of our victories. We are also able to evaluate our progress and be encouraged by all the wonder in our life.

Right now, take a moment and fill in the following sample pages taken from Receive Joy's Daily Asking Journal and Inspiration Notebook available on www.receivejoy.com or Amazon.

Journaling

GOALS FOR THIS YEAR

_____

_____

_____

_____

_____

_____

_____

_____

_____

_____

_____

_____

I vividly see myself with my goals obtained and miracles created!

_____   _____
Signature   Date

Connect To The Light

MY MONTHLY GOALS

My goals for the month of _____

_____
_____
_____
_____
_____
_____
_____
_____
_____
_____
_____

I vividly see myself with my goals obtained and miracles created!

_____   _____
Signature   Date

Journaling

Date: _____

***I now joyfully accept and appreciate the abundant life
the Universe offers me.***

I am grateful for:	What may I do to allow more happiness and peace in my life?
_____	_____
_____	_____
_____	**I have fun and celebrate this day by:**
_____	_____

I ask with focused intent for:	Why?
_____	_____
_____	_____
_____	_____
_____	_____
_____	_____
_____ and more!	_____

My gains and miracles created:	
_____	1 _____
_____	2 _____
_____	3 _____
_____	4 _____
_____	5 _____

To God be the glory!   Thank you for my breath of life.   I rejoice always.

"Rejoice in the Lord always: and again I say, Rejoice."
—Philippians 4:4 (KJV)

- ❏ I read my Bible.
- ❏ I am connected to God.
- ❏ I meditated for 15 min.
- ❏ I edited my words three times.
- ❏ I prayed.
- ❏ I smile.

☺

second energy ▢

Connect To The Light

GAINS, SUCCESSES, AND MIRACLES RECEIVED

_____
_____
_____
_____
_____
_____
_____
_____
_____
_____
_____
_____
_____
_____
_____

Chapter 15

LIVE BY DESIGN

Step One is to connect, plug in and turn on, check our connection, and reconnect several times throughout the day. **Let us make sure the power is flowing from the source into us in order for us to receive**. Are we connected?

Being intentionally connected to the Source Light Energy enables us to live by design. To live by design is to take ownership of our life, our choices, and our attitude. It is time to master our happiness, health, wealth, and finances. Let us have an active motivating plan, be in constant co-creation, and choose positivity. Actively incorporate ways to connect and stay connected to the light into our daily walk. Living by design is practical, experiential, and fun!

Connect To The Light

Let us know our life's mission, investigate ourself, pray, contemplate, read our Bible, be in community, flow with nature, receive joy, contribute, and journal. These are all wonderful methods to co-create with God. Everyone can absolutely do this and work with the Creator of all there is. In this chapter, Receive Joy offers six more suggestions that can help us to stay connected and keep our eyes on the victory:

1. Make Known Your Heart
2. Positive Words
3. Reminders
4. Focus Target
5. Focus Wheel
6. Abundance

1—Make Known Your Heart

When we are ordering a pizza, we tell the person taking our order our exact desires. Let us just be aware that our life is like a pizza order, every day and every hour. It is amazing to note that if we really were specific with our personal pizza order, then when many pizzas are lined up on the counter, we can immediately recognize ours.

Live By Design

> *Thank You, God.*
> *I know this is my pizza. It is exactly what I ordered. I planned out and formulated that order and it matches exactly. As there are other pizzas belonging to other people, I recognize mine instantly.*

There may have been many years when we just sat down and talked to our friends and placed few personal orders. Oftentimes our joy may leave us when our pizza shows up in a less than desired state, or we have been waiting too long for it to arrive.

In that case, we were living less than "by design" and by our feelings. Life showed us that there is a gap between what we really desired and what we received. We had this idea in our heart and our head how life might be; however, the reality proved to be less satisfying or different from our expectations. Possibly we had yet to check that we were connected, harnessed on, plugged in, and turned on. Our pen had been left in the drawer and our journal empty. Was there even a journal?

Connect To The Light

God is a very accurate God. This Universe is meticulously and accurately designed. One thing leads to another that leads to another, and it all flows together in synchronicity. The same holds true for the macrocosm and microcosm. When we look at our own bodies, we see that everything works together in unity. All the organ systems are functioning together and relying on each other in a constant flow. Even when we are asleep, our cells are developing, reproducing, recharging, and healing.

God set this Universe up with absolute accuracy. He planned everything from the beginning to the end. We are His children, and if our orders are yet to come, we still have to **set ourself up to be conscious enough to recognize and receive** them. Do we trust ourselves to receive? Do we believe that we are worthy? Do we believe that God loves us so much as His chosen children that He wishes to deliver? We hold His creation power and we walk in His authority. He wishes for us to plan and live by design, using the power He has placed in this Universe during creation, the same power we harness and use by our spoken and written words that co-create everything. Thus, have pen and paper and begin journaling like all the great minds did before us. I own a huge book that contains only a fraction of Leonardo da Vinci's sketches, drawings, notes, journal entries, and ideas—all written down. The world was left with over 1,500 notebooks from Thomas Edison. In a time when the camera was yet to be invented, drawing sketches was a way of capturing magnificent ideas. Similarly, let us capture our ideas and thoughts. Record some greatness every day on paper. We too are inventors, artists, poets, and writers. Let us open up to and welcome in our creativity. How many journals and workbooks do we have on our shelf that we penned?

When we are connected, we automatically take part in creating. We move forward to order every part of our life. Every day we place orders and receive deliveries. It is up to us to decide to order consciously and with focus, thus influencing what we receive and ultimately our life. Know what pizza we wish to order before we even sit down.

Did we pen all our orders? Have we defined our orders? Let us always order our own pizza, with all our own delicious toppings that we wish for in this life. Organize a purposeful life on paper. Or guess what we will have for dinner? Other people's orders. Many of us have eaten a lot of other people's orders. We ate our parent's orders, we ate our friend's orders, we maybe ate orders from people we shared an intimate relationship with. Some people have separated because they have had enough of that order. If we are more aware and put more parameters around our personal orders, then we can live a fulfilled, happy life. We have to know what we desire. We are doing everybody a favor when we know what we wish for, in life and in our relationships. It is best for everyone if we take the time to express ourself and preorder.

I was out to lunch with a dear friend. She took a moment to preorder her deli meat. She calls the deli and orders everything so when she arrives they have it all ready to be picked up instead of waiting in line.

In the past we may have waited in line. Why? We can preorder and simply say "Thank you" and pick it all up. Everything is ready for us.

God loves preorders! He loves to use the whole Universe to have our orders waiting for us. It is done, so when we walk in, our order is prepared for us. This is true connection: When we make our heart known, when we are constantly preordering with detail and our life is lived by proactive, purposeful design.

For my 10-month trip around the world, I took a whole stack of prayers from all my friends with me to pray over them everywhere I went, and to leave them at the Wailing Wall in Jerusalem toward the end of my trip.

Once in Jerusalem, I waited to visit the Wailing

Wall until the last day, when I received the inspired thought to go there at once. At the Wailing Wall, I was looking around for an opening large enough to fit my whole stack of papers. As a professional asker and educator, I had more and larger papers than the tiny pieces other people put in the small spaces between the bricks. Eventually, I saw a brick missing and put the whole stack there, praying over the nation of Israel, as well as all the prayers I had brought with me. I was praying that our beautiful handwritten prayers will stay neat and orderly for God to enjoy. After I left the Wailing Wall, our tour guide received a call with a notification that the Wailing Wall was to be closed within the hour for the ritual of collecting, praying over, and burying all prayers according to Jewish tradition. This ritual happens twice a year. Once before Passover in the spring and once in the fall before the Jewish New Year. Our prayers stayed preserved and were blessed within the hour I placed them there. God is very precise.

2—Positive Words

Every word is a creation. We can choose to create love, joy, gratitude, hope, compassion, mercy, praise, and much more positivity with our words—or we can choose to create the lack thereof.

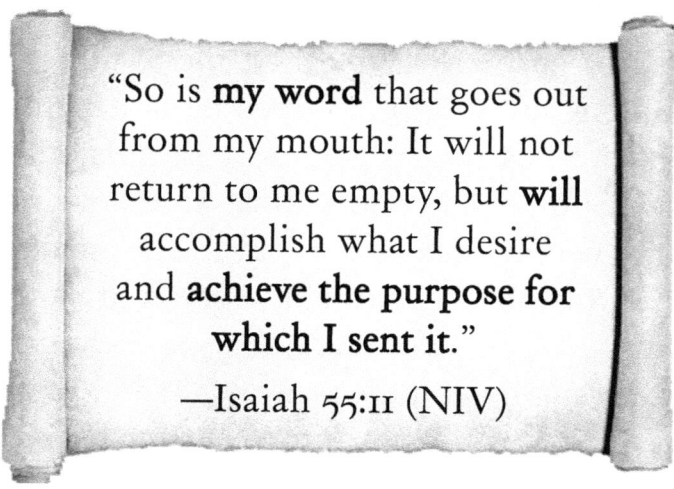

"So is **my word** that goes out from my mouth: It will not return to me empty, but **will** accomplish what I desire and **achieve the purpose for which I sent it.**"
—Isaiah 55:11 (NIV)

Are our words supporting our purpose? Let us be conscious of which words we send out to achieve what we desire. Our words come from our thoughts. If we simply listen to our own words, we can tell how positive our thoughts are in every moment.

I once had a salesperson come to my house to demonstrate a piece of equipment in which I was interested. She said that the equipment is so good that she does "*not need*" to sell it to me, she is just here to share the greatness of it. I replied, "Wow! This is interesting. Then I will have to call someone else, because I am ready to buy this piece of equipment." She thought for a moment and said, "Oh, what I really mean is, I am happy to sell it to you. That is what I am here for." I advised her to declare her desired outcome by choosing her words carefully.

A couple months later, she and her business partner told me that they had been wondering why they had so many people showing interest in the product, yet sales were lower than expected. They were asking for the reason and then they met me the same week. This was a huge "aha" moment, when **they first became conscious about the words they were using** to sell their product and what they were teaching in their sales trainings. Changing their words made a big difference and significantly increased their closing rate.

Ask yourself:

What words can I change to improve my outcome?

Connect To The Light

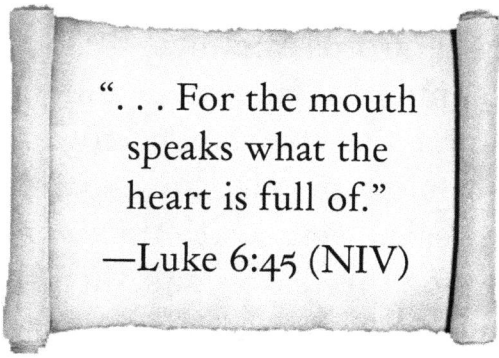

"... For the mouth speaks what the heart is full of."
—Luke 6:45 (NIV)

Please ask yourself:

Are my words defining me?

Am I conscious and aware of my own words?

Do I understand the power of my own words?

Am I encouraging myself and others with every word I speak?

When I first came to the United States for an internship position and learned English, I was very impressed with the positive replies I received when I offered someone a "Thank you." There were warm smiles and phrases such as "my pleasure" and "you are welcome." Being born in Berlin, Germany, where eye-contact and kindness were rather rare, I felt very welcomed, and these responses also quickly became a habit in my vocabulary. Returning home, studying in northern Germany, I made being welcoming and nice to everyone a priority that surely received recognition and trained me well for my service on cruise ships. I am grateful that I learned in my early twenties that I have a choice of the words I use, and the demeanor I present. After eight years, I came back to Naples and noticed that the responses to "Thank you" have changed. Now, I am frequently handed *"no problem," "no worries,"* and *"I don't blame you."* What happened to our language? I certainly pray for a revival of positive manners and positive word choices. This is the reason I advocate for the Power of Positive Words.

Positive thoughts become positive words to ourself, as well as to others. Positive messages fill our heart with goodness, gladness, and joy. If our use of positive words requires further development, this may show that our thoughts yearn for conscious enhancement. Let us revitalize our thoughts. Choose positivity over what movies, media, the Internet, and the world offer us.

Connect To The Light

In the beginning was the Word. We can start by rediscovering all the good words and train our minds to use expanded positive vocabulary. Let us always speak kind words of abundance. To some of us it may feel like learning a new language. This new language is conscious creation.

Let us extend our vocabulary. We tend to use the same words and phrases over and over. Make it a game. Every new positive word we bring into our thoughts brings joy, peace, and happiness with it.

Write down all the words you can think of in exchange for good and amazing.

Live By Design

Now that we have such a wonderful list of beautiful positive words, there is plenty for which we can use it:

- ♥ Read these words out loud to imprint ourself
- ♥ Write them on our water bottle or water pitcher to imprint our water
- ♥ Use them when we describe experiences
- ♥ Use them in our daily correspondence: add them to emails and texts we send
- ♥ Meditate on these words and be open to the feelings they induce

Receive Joy also started a list, and here is what I came up with. Feel free to add some of these words to your list and email me (ask@receivejoy.com) if I can add words to my list.

abundant	advanced
accelerating	advantageous
accurate	affectionate
achieving	affirmative
acknowledgeable	aligned
admirable	alive
adorable	alluring

Connect To The Light

altruistic	bright
amiable	brilliant
amusing	celestial
angelic	charismatic
anticipated	charming
appealing	cheerful
appreciated	cherished
artistic	classy
astonishing	clear
astounding	clever
attractive	colorful
awakening	comfortable
awe-inspiring	compassionate
awesome	compelling
beaming	complete
beautiful	conscious
bedazzling	courageous
beneficial	courteous
best	creative
beyond	curious
blessed	dazzling
blissful	deep
blooming	delicate
bountiful	delicious
brave	delightful

desirable	essential
distinguished	established
divine	eternal
dynamic	ethereal
easy	everlasting
ecstatic	exalted
effective	excellent
efficient	exceptional
elated	exciting
elegant	exemplary
elite	exhilarating
emotional	exquisite
empowering	extraordinary
encouraging	exuberant
energetic	eye-opening
energizing	fabulous
engaging	faithful
engrossing	fancy
enigmatic	fantastic
enjoyable	fascinating
enriching	favorable
entertaining	favored
enthralling	fetching
enticing	first-class
epic	first-rate

Connect To The Light

flattering	honest
flourishing	honorable
fruitful	humorous
fulfilling	iconic
fun	ideal
generous	imaginative
genius	important
genuine	impressive
gifted	industrious
gleaming	ingenious
glittering	innovative
glorifying	insightful
glorious	inspiring
golden	intelligent
gorgeous	interesting
gracious	intuitive
grand	inventive
gratifying	inviting
great	joyous
gripping	kindhearted
ground-breaking	laudable
headline-worthy	legendary
heartwarming	light
heavenly	likable
helpful	life-giving

lovely	perfect
lucrative	phenomenal
luminous	pioneering
luscious	pitch-perfect
magical	pivotal
magnanimous	pleasant
magnetic	pleasing
magnificent	positive
majestic	powerful
marvelous	precious
masterful	preeminent
meaningful	preferable
meritorious	prime
mesmerizing	proactive
mighty	prodigious
mind-changing	profitable
mindful	profound
miraculous	prominent
monumental	propitious
neat	prosperous
notable	purpose-giving
nourishing	quintessential
optimistic	radiant
outstanding	rapturous
peaceful	rare

Connect To The Light

ravishing	stellar
real	sterling
refined	stirring
refreshing	striking
remarkable	strong
renewing	stunning
reputable	sublime
resourceful	successful
resplendent	suitable
rewarding	super
rich	superb
righteous	supporting
riveting	supreme
satisfying	surprising
sensational	tantalizing
sensual	tasteful
sharp	tempting
significant	thought-provoking
smart	thrilling
solid	top-notch
soulful	touching
sparkling	trailblazing
special	transcendent
splendid	transformational
startling	tremendous

Live By Design

triumphant	well chosen
trusting	well done
truthful	well known
unique	wholesome
uplifting	wise
useful	wonderful
valuable	wondrous
vibrant	world-class
victorious	worthy
vital	

I also keep a growing list of beautiful positive words to actively enhance my vocabulary.

Start your own beautiful word list in your journal.

Refer to the list in Receive Joy's Ask And You Shall Receive book, pages 91 to 101, or email Receive Joy for a free copy (ask@receivejoy.com).

Connect To The Light

One of our Miracle Group members uses the word list in the book to enhance her text as she writes her emails.

> *Copy the words and put them near your desk. Actively incorporate them into your daily communication.*

Receive Joy recorded a CD full of *Beautiful Words* to play in the car or background to increase our active vocabulary of positive words and to bless us and our environment. The frequencies of these words clear the air, soothe our pets, and imprint water (in our body, in our plants, in our pets, in our bottles, and in our pipes).

Let us read and write positive affirmations. Anything we do repetitively anchors in our mind and becomes part of our habitual patterning. Anchoring helps to form new neural pathways. Affirming with words and actions at the same time is the most powerful anchoring. If we speak our affirmations while being physically active, for example as we are walking, jogging, rebounding, or tapping, they are anchored even deeper.

Let us use physical anchoring to strengthen our affirmations. Be aware of every word in our affirmations. Every word counts. Please make sure they are entirely positive and beautiful. To help *Receive Inspiration,* Receive Joy created a CD of positive affirmations.

Here are examples of positive beautiful affirmations:

- ♥ I am beautiful inside and out
- ♥ I am privileged with constant awareness
- ♥ I live each day as if it is the best day of my life
- ♥ I am connected to the light
- ♥ I receive inspiration, new ideas, well-being, and beauty
- ♥ I expand my mind with beautiful words
- ♥ My life is light and easy
- ♥ I am awesome
- ♥ I am a true blessing to this world
- ♥ I am worthy, and I deserve it

- ♥ I keep on smiling
- ♥ God has blessed me
- ♥ All is good all the time
- ♥ Joy is mine forevermore
- ♥ Love and gratitude continue to flow to me
- ♥ I live in the now, rejoicing always
- ♥ I love myself

Anchoring also takes place when we share our stories on. Let us set all our *sad* stories down on God's altar for good. Let us be aware to only share the encouraging words and positive stories we wish to have imprinted in our mind and re-created in our life. Living by design includes using positive, encouraging words all the time.

3—Reminders

Reminders that we strategically place everywhere help us to stay connected. We can put something in the car or on our desk that will remind us to connect; for example, a sticky note with a Bible verse or a cheerful saying, a cross, our Bible, etc. In the bathroom, we can put a similar reminder:

Live By Design

An encouraging saying, an uplifting poem, a happy picture, or a gratitude stone. Everywhere we go, let us put reminders of our connection. Wear a necklace with a cross, a heart, a charm, a crystal. Every time our eyes meet these reminders, we smile and these items make us remember to check our connection and to reconnect. Here are other examples of reminders to connect that may help us to succeed in greatness:

- ♥ Have a morning routine including the first conscious thought of "Here I am, God."
- ♥ Set up reminders/alarms on the phone
- ♥ Attend church and Bible Study
- ♥ Put up signs, such as "This is a house of prayer."
- ♥ Have a prayer space or connection corner
- ♥ Pray over our food at every meal
- ♥ Pray for a successful outcome before every meeting and before making decisions
- ♥ Pray before we start driving
- ♥ Pray before we answer the phone or dial a number

Connect To The Light

> *Here I am God. Here I am God. Here I am God. I love You.*

I have reminders to connect all over my house. I have a Jesus doll on my bathroom counter that is holding a small blonde doll (me) and the Tree of Life. I have a picture of Akiane's Jesus portrait on my desk. I have a Bible by the entrance door. I am reminded to connect every time I leave my house and when I come home. I am reminded when I brush my teeth and wash my hands.

I love to see how others stay connected. One of my friends leaves her hymn book open on her piano. Every time she walks by, she is reminded to connect and has a beautiful song on her mind. I walked into a friend's house and she has her reading glasses purposefully laid on her Bible. Every time she is looking for her glasses, she is reminded to read the Bible.

These are great examples of how to live by purposeful design.

4—Focus Target

Humans produce massive energy. Visualize us shooting energy arrows all day long from the moment our eyes open until we close them for the night. Once we direct our energy arrows toward our focus targets and keep our eyes on the victory, we will achieve our goals. To keep our eyes on the victory, let us write our most important goal in the center of the bull's-eye on the Focus Target. Fill in other desires according to their importance in the outer rings. After the whole target is filled in, a copy can be placed where we can see it daily. When we have a target, our energy arrows have purposeful aim.

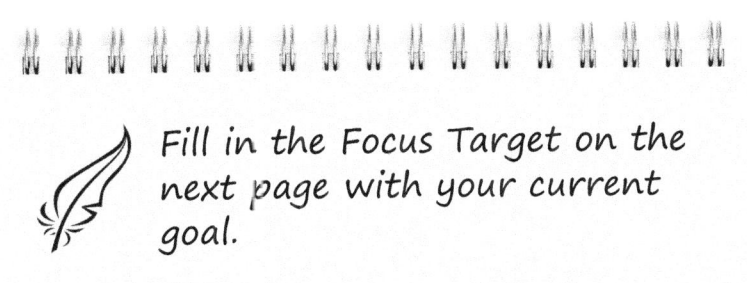

Fill in the Focus Target on the next page with your current goal.

Connect To The Light

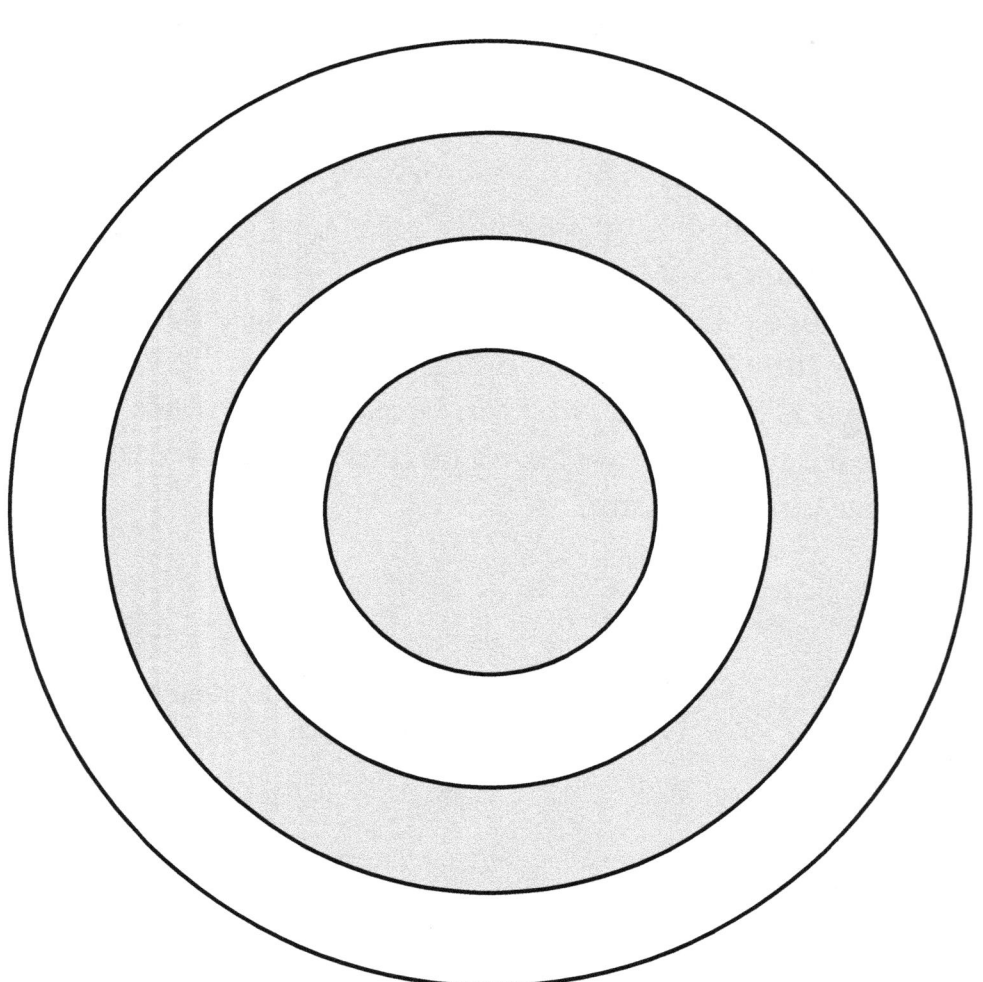

5—Focus Wheel

The Focus Wheel aids us to build confidence and be courageous. Let us list all the reasons that we can have our goal. As we increase our belief, the desired outcome is attainable. We are creating solid evidence to increase our belief and ultimately receive our desired goal.

Write a positive affirmation in the middle of the circle on page 219. It is a statement you wish to increase your faith about. It is praying in writing.

Example: I am worthy of God's love.

Now fill in the spokes of the wheel by writing what you already can believe about this statement and all solution-oriented actions.

For example:

♥ I am God's child

♥ Jesus died for me

Connect To The Light

- ♥ Other people are confident about their worthiness; so am I
- ♥ God tells me so in the Bible
- ♥ I know God loves and supports me
- ♥ I connect to the light constantly
- ♥ The whole Bible is a love letter full of encouragement to humanity and personally to me
- ♥ I deserve God's fatherly love
- ♥ He promised that I am worthy
- ♥ God's mercy and grace abound

Now, choose your own statement or use this example to fill in the following blank Focus Wheel.

Receive Joy offers a *Focus Wheel Workbook* (see page 259) that aids in increasing over fifty common beliefs.

Live By Design

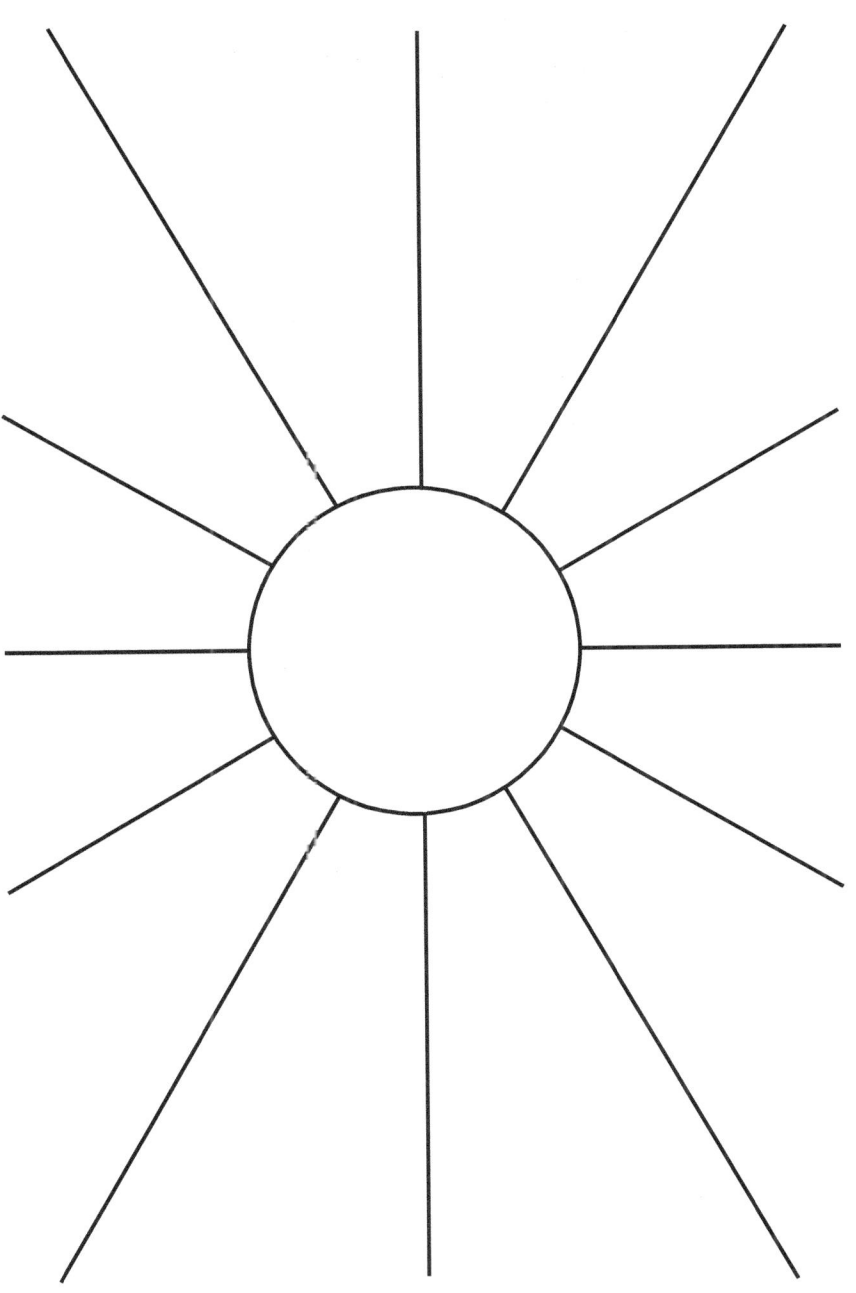

6—Abundance

Let us decide to use God's miraculous light and implement it in our daily walk. Live by design! God wishes for us to prosper and live abundantly.

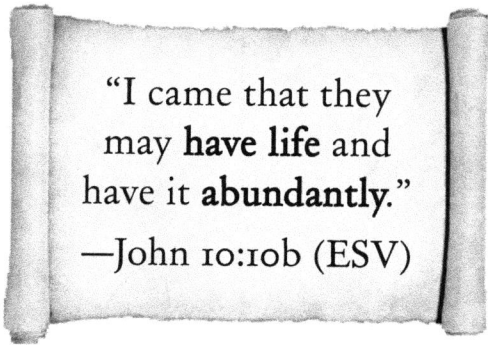

"I came that they may **have life** and have it **abundantly**."
—John 10:10b (ESV)

Live By Design

Please ask yourself:

Am I living an okay life or do I live prosperously and abundantly?

Ok   Abundantly
(circle the answer you wish to live by)

What does it mean to live abundantly in my existence right now?

_____

_____

_____

_____

Connect To The Light

 Use the Five Minute Couch Time to investigate if you feel any blockage or resistance in your belief system that causes you to live less than abundantly:

Is the belief I hold still benefitting me?

Yes   No   (circle the answer)

Where does the belief system come from?

Does it come from a family member, a teacher, a friend, society, religion, etc.?

_____

_____

Is it truly my belief I am living in?

Yes   No   (circle the answer)

Do I wish to replace this belief with one that serves me better?

Yes   No   (circle the answer)

Live By Design

Can I replace this belief right now?

Yes   No   (circle the answer)

What new empowering belief serves me better?

_____

_____

_____

_____

You may wish to do a Focus Wheel with your new belief system in the center. Use the blank Focus Wheel on the next page. Fill in the spokes of the wheel by writing what you already can believe about this statement and solution-oriented actions.

Connect To The Light

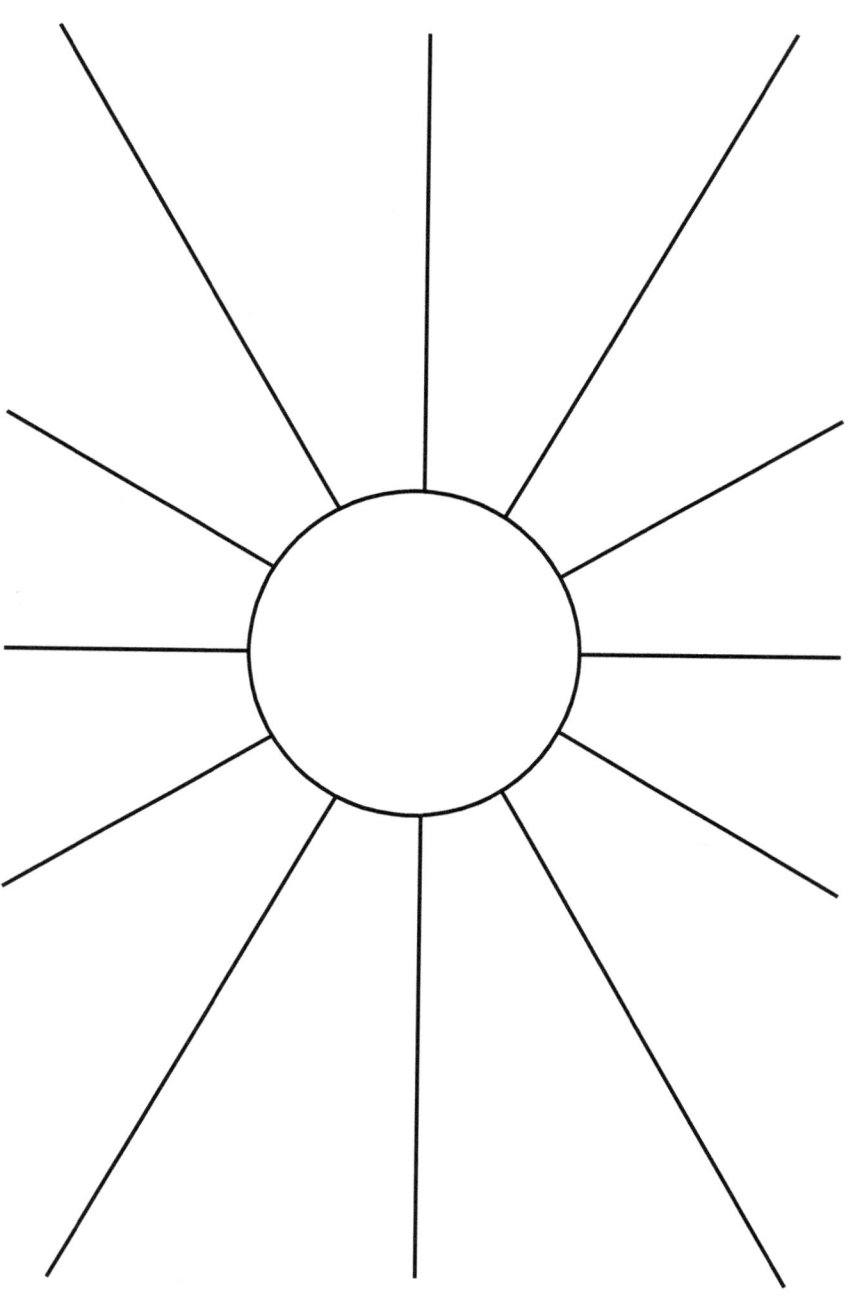

Live By Design

For example: I live my life abundantly

- ♥ It is God's promise to me
- ♥ God tells me so in the Bible
- ♥ I am God's child
- ♥ There is abundance everywhere
- ♥ I have more than enough air to breathe
- ♥ I always have more than enough
- ♥ The best things in life are free and abundant
- ♥ Other people live abundantly; so can I
- ♥ I pray and present my petitions before God
- ♥ I ask more to receive more
- ♥ I journal
- ♥ I educate myself about any area in which I wish to increase my abundance

Let us harness on to God's belief system, His word, and His promises. Let us focus on His power. Let us have faith and joy in Him. This is our opportunity to be harnessed to God alone and to be filled with the light to which we are connected. Let us become more transparent by focusing our eyes on God alone.

Connect To The Light

When we polish ourself up by honoring God and His power placed in each of us, we become transparent, allowing God's light to shine through us. We share the light through our good works. Now we are able to give and receive in true abundance.

Chapter 16

BE THE LIGHT

On my recent trip to Norway, I visited a tiny church that had colorful stained-glass windows depicting images of saints. The preacher told a story of a little girl who asked her grandmother what saints are. As she sat through the service, she noticed the beams of sunlight shining through the stained-glass windows of the saints over all the people. On the way home from church, she said to her grandmother, "Now I know what saints are. They are the people who allow God's light to shine through them onto all the people of the world."

> "You are the light of the world. A city that is set on a hill cannot be hidden. Nor do they light a lamp and put it under a basket, but on a lampstand, and it gives light to all who are in the house. **Let your light so shine before men, that they may see your good works and glorify your Father in heaven.**"
>
> —Matthew 5:14-16 (NKJV)

God's light contains all goodness, love, grace, mercy, forgiveness, wisdom, power, patience, joy, comfort, strength, hope, truth, glory, justice, righteousness, redemption, salvation, etc.

What does it mean to be the light? It means to **be heavenly minded, yet of earthly use**. This begins by being good, gentle, kind, and loving toward ourself first, speaking kind words of encouragement and strength. This opens us up to allow God's light

Be The Light

to shine through us and **do many good works**: Be positive, speak beautiful words that show our good thoughts and our good heart, give, help, be a good parent and love our children, be a good neighbor, be a good friend, be kind, be patient, be accepting, be a helpful spouse, and be a cheerful giver. Be rich in good works to ourself and others. Let us keep our light out in the open to shine brightly and for everyone to see. We are made to shine brightly so that we can do good works.

> "For we are God's handiwork, created in Christ Jesus to **do good works**, which God prepared in advance for us to do."
> —Ephesians 2:10 (NIV)

"... **whoever practices the truth comes into the Light,** so that it may be seen clearly that what he has done has been accomplished in God."

—John 3:21 (NIV)

"For you were once darkness, but now you are light in the Lord. **Live as children of light** ... (for the fruit of the light consists in all goodness, righteousness and truth) and find out what pleases the Lord. ... everything exposed by the light becomes visible— and **everything that is illuminated becomes a light.**"

—Ephesians 5:8-13 (NIV)

Be The Light

What is our standard? Is aligning with the Lord our standard or is pleasing others our priority? What type of approval is most important to us? Let us ask ourself if our thoughts, words, and deeds are pleasing to God. God's understanding of all things is so much greater than our own. Ultimately, God's approval is all that counts. Connect with Jesus! Call on His glorious name. There is power in His name. Jesus is the light of the world.

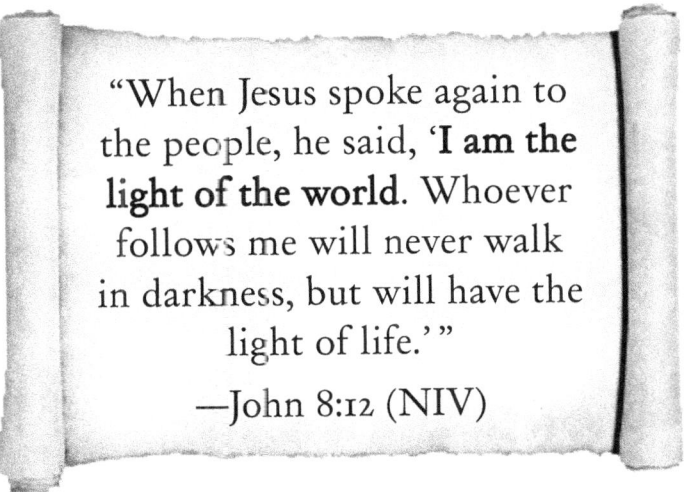

"When Jesus spoke again to the people, he said, '**I am the light of the world.** Whoever follows me will never walk in darkness, but will have the light of life.'"
—John 8:12 (NIV)

If you have Christ, you have the light to be the light. Jesus is the eternal light and we are colorful polished glass illuminated by His light. God first created light, then he created us to be beacons of light. Because we are made in His image, we are born

Connect To The Light

of His light, we are filled with light, we are activated by light, and we are one with His light.

Let us find true light in Christ and spend more time in the light of God. The closer we are to His light, the brighter we can shine. Instead of asking how much can I become like the Lord, our question shall be: How much of the world can I embrace, enjoy, and engage in, and still be connected to His light?

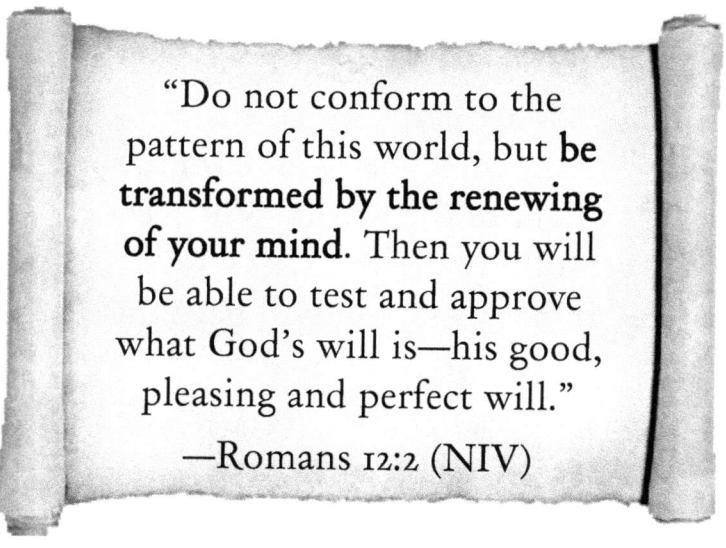

"Do not conform to the pattern of this world, but **be transformed by the renewing of your mind.** Then you will be able to test and approve what God's will is—his good, pleasing and perfect will."

—Romans 12:2 (NIV)

Let us surrender and allow God's true light to shine through us. **We shall live our life as lighthouses, from which beams of heavenly light shine out into the world.** Be His light, keep on shining and live as true children of light. Once we are lit, we can go forth and light the world. Let us make an illuminating difference in our world and be the light.

Our experience on Earth is an opportunity for each of us to investigate our inner being and choose to be a light. Receive Joy's desire is for humanity to be the light of love, joy, peace, patience, kindness, goodness, faithfulness, gentleness, and self-control, as this is the fruit, the pouring forth, of the Holy Spirit (Galatians 5:22-23, ESV).

I wish for each of us to **be a bright light so that we can light others**, one candle (person) at a time. Let us be conscious of our thoughts and our words. Let us be rightminded so that God's light of truth is bright and illuminating as it flows through us and is passed on.

The following story is an account from one of our Miracle Group members: My vision is to share the information I received from Receive Joy with the youth. I was doing my contemplation in the morning and I received this very strong nudge to give the book *Ask And You Shall Receive* to my friend in Wisconsin who is about my age. I gave it to her and she loved it. We talked about it. She really wished to join our Miracle Group online or start one of her own up north. Her daughter, who has just graduated from college and had gone off to Philadelphia on her own, was being challenged finding the right friends. My friend loved the content of the book and used it in her own life, thus she bought a copy on Amazon for her daughter.

A couple of months later, when I was back in Florida, I received this strong nudge in contemplation to also give the workbook to my friend. I am using the *Daily Asking Journal*, so I purchased the workbook for her. She was very excited again. "This is so great. This is making a huge difference in my life. It is already making a significant difference in my daughter's life. I am also buying the journal for her and sending it to her."

A year later, my husband and I were sitting in a coffee shop, when all of a sudden, in walks the daughter. It is the first time I saw her in four years. And she was very excited and surprised to see me: "Is that you? I was just now telling my boyfriend about you."

Being in her early twenties, she was so ready for all this information. She told me it totally changed her life. She thanked me repeatedly. Now, I am passing this Thank You on to Receive Joy. She said, "I journal every day. Over the past year I have been experiencing miracle after miracle. Meet my boyfriend. He is a miracle." And now, even her boyfriend is opening up to all the possibilities God has to offer.

Be The Light

My vision is to put all of the tools and information into the hands and hearts of our youth, so that they choose positivity and joy to live an amazing life full of light. For me, it is all about being excited about life and doing something exciting with our life. I wished for my friend to be excited, she wished for her daughter to be excited, and now, all of us are lit up even more.

We charge our cellphone, plug in the toaster and the hairdryer, so let us also plug our life in first. Whatever we use, let us power it up first. Live by design. Let us harness God's power so that we ourself shall be power-full. Once we are connected and powered up, our good works are multiplied.

Look up. Look up at the sky. There stretched out is the almighty power source: Our triune God and His Universe, full of everlasting energy. This is also where the heavenly hosts are: God's angels. We can call on all of this energy instantly. Live by conscious design, call on God's Power regularly, throughout the day, throughout the night, and every time our eyes open. First, seek Him first, and **connect to the Light**.

Connect To The Light

"... let us **walk in the light** of the LORD."
—Isaiah 2:5 (KJV)

REDISCOVER TRUTH and *Receive Joy*

CONNECT TO THE LIGHT

> "Seek ye **first** the Kingdom of Heaven (God) and his righteousness; and all these things shall be added unto you."
>
> —Matthew 6:33 (KJV)

We charge our cellphone, plug in the toaster and the hairdryer, let us also plug our life in first. Step one in the process of truly deciding to make changes in our life and begin living by design starts with the understanding that we are connected to the greatest Power Source there is—God. Let us **consciously connect first** and **harness this power**. Once we are connected our life starts to flow.

Happy New Day Prayer To Connect First

Happy new day, God. Here I am. I thank You! I praise You! God, You are the source of light in my life. I recognize Your good that is abundant everywhere. Align our wills. I am holding my journal in my hands and I am praying to You. Oh God, bless me indeed and enlarge my territory. Keep Your hand upon me. You have my heart written down! Yes, I welcome in all these things to be added to my life. Thank You, Lord. I love You.

My Divine Mission is _____

_____
_____
_____
_____
_____
_____
_____
_____
_____
_____

Ways To Connect And Stay Connected

- ♥ I seek God's kingdom first. Here I am, God.
- ♥ I connect with my breath.
- ♥ I have a current Divine Mission Statement.
- ♥ I know my gifts and talents and use them.
- ♥ I know what is beyond the Grand Doors of my life.
- ♥ I receive joy. I know what is fun for me.
- ♥ I constantly collect data on myself. I have current Who Am I and My Ideal Self lists.
- ♥ I feel the connection.
- ♥ I pray and personally communicate with God.
- ♥ I ask in prayer and petition with thanksgiving. I approach God in confidence.
- ♥ I meditate daily and listen to God.
- ♥ I own a Bible. I read The Holy Bible and I am inspired by His Word.
- ♥ I am in community.
- ♥ I flow with nature. I give and receive.
- ♥ I contribute. I am a cheerful giver.
- ♥ I journal daily.
- ♥ I live by conscious design and make my heart known to God.
- ♥ I am focused on my goals. I have annual, monthly, weekly, and daily goals. I know what I desire now.
- ♥ I ask in detail and leave the "how" to God.
- ♥ I use the power of positive words. My thoughts attract and my words create.

- ♥ I am the matching and attracting vibration to good. I reap what I sow.
- ♥ I use constant reminders to connect.
- ♥ I have faith. I increase my belief in all areas that require enhancement.
- ♥ I am polished so that God's light can shine brightly through me.
- ♥ I am the light.

Connect To The Light provides ways to maintain our connection to the light energy and to live by conscious design. Let us be heavenly minded, yet of earthly use.

> ". . . let us **walk in the light** of the LORD."
> —Isaiah 2:5 (KJV)

CONNECT TO THE LIGHT

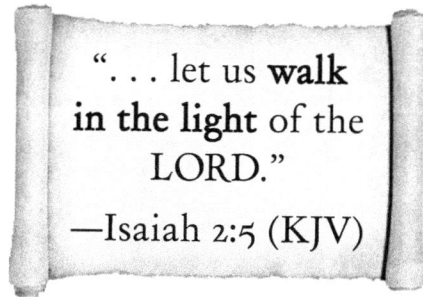

Rediscover Truth

(239) 450-1240
ask@receivejoy.com
www.receivejoy.com

The Nine Steps To Conscious Creation

1. **Connect**: Plug into God's Almighty **Gift**, the Power of the Universe, and discover your life's purpose.
2. **Declare**: Be clear about what you are truly seeking, and ask for it.
   Have **Faith,** focus, and be courageous.
3. **Dominate**: Receive your inheritance and put on your crown.
   Believe.
4. **Be calm**: **Align** your head with your heart.
   Have **Peace**.
5. **Take action**: Focus on your breath and let the "how" be up to God.
   Let Him wow us with the "how." He does it.
6. **Lead with love**: Let us **love ourself first**.
   Have **Grace**.
7. **Bless everyone** and **everything** with **love and gratitude**.
   Have **Mercy**.
8. **Expect the miracle in every moment**. Know the **Truth**.
   Be conscious of what you create and allow yourself to receive your desires.
9. **Have fun and celebrate**: Enjoy your creation and rejoice.
   Trust God.

Date: _____

I now joyfully accept and appreciate the abundant life the Universe offers me.

I am grateful for:	What may I do to allow more happiness and peace in my life?
_____	_____
_____	_____
_____	
_____	I have fun and celebrate this day by:
	_____
	_____

I ask with focused intent for:	Why?
_____	_____
_____	_____
_____	_____
_____	_____
_____	_____
_____ and more!	_____

My gains and miracles created:	
_____	1 _____
_____	2 _____
_____	3 _____
_____	4 _____
_____	5 _____

To God be the glory!   Thank you for my breath of life.   I rejoice always.

"Rejoice in the Lord always: and again I say, Rejoice."
—Philippians 4:4 (KJV)

- ❏ I read my Bible.
- ❏ I am connected to God.
- ❏ I meditated for 15 min.
- ❏ I edited my words three times.
- ❏ I prayed.
- ❏ I smile.

☺

second energy ☐

Notes

Notes

Notes

Notes

Notes

Notes

Notes

Notes

Notes

Notes

ACKNOWLEDGMENTS

With Love and Gratitude, we give our heartfelt thanks to the following:

- ♥ God, Jesus, and the Holy Spirit, for guiding us with Your inspiration and content of this book
- ♥ Ourselves, for our dedicated focus and love to complete the book for all humanity
- ♥ Our families and friends, for their continual love
- ♥ Everyone in our Miracle Group and Million True Millionaires: All the beautiful, positive people who shared their joy and their creation stories and who always are a delight to be around
- ♥ Steve Jones, for the beautiful picture of a rainbow around the sun. He captured that moment while visiting the Hogar de Ninos Nazareth orphanage in Honduras with his favorite charity, All God's Children. The rainbow was in the sky for about six hours and everyone viewed this as a sign from God that He was blessing their work
- ♥ Tom Messina, for the book cover. He masterfully transformed Steve's picture into a

front cover and added his own cloud pictures to enhance the back cover. His graphic design work for Receive Joy is outstanding

- ♥ Christine Perry. Her first read-through of the book enriched its concepts, as she is constantly reminding us of the audience for whom we write and to include the fundamentals for a light and easy reading experience

- ♥ Barbara Compagnucci, for proof-reading the manuscript, and placing the commas where they belong

- ♥ James Subramanian, for creating a beautiful book out of a manuscript

- ♥ Joey Madia, for editing *Connect To The Light* and narrating the audiobook

- ♥ And everyone who read *Ask And You Shall Receive* and uses the *Daily Asking Journal* and the *Inspiration Notebook*. Thank you for all the encouragement, testimonies, and miracle stories we received from you. If we are yet to meet you, please email Receive Joy at ask@receivejoy.com to add you to our prayer and newsletter list

May God continue to bless us all.

MILLION TRUE MILLIONAIRES

MTM is a social network bringing together an international community of positive, purpose-driven individuals who strive for growth, contribution, and love.

This is your personal invitation to join the MTM community for an annual fee of $225, to:

- ♥ Have access to other members—what a joy it is to have like-minded, purpose-driven individuals with whom to connect
- ♥ Share your visions and askings and start receiving
- ♥ Market your products and services
- ♥ Find new business partners and make friends
- ♥ Receive mentorship from proven successful individuals

- ♥ Browse the library to find empowering videos, e-books, and links to amazing websites and blogs

- ♥ Receive regular newsletters and invitations to webinars in which we share valuable information to help you and your business grow

- ♥ Receive Community and Encouragement. Our goal is for all MTM members to succeed together as we encourage each other along the way. We all grow abundantly in happiness, health, and wealth

- ♥ Receive Love and Prayer. All our members are constantly prayed over

Tap into all of these benefits and become part of this success network. People who are successful have one thing in common: They believe that they can succeed and so they do. MTM is here to support its members. Together, we share in each other's greatness. We each wish to experience and spread community, love, kindness, positivity, personal growth, peace on earth, bettering of humankind, charity, giving, and receiving.

With blessings in Abundance, your MTM Family
A Family of Wealth—We trust in God!

www.milliontruemillionaires.com

AVAILABLE FROM RECEIVE JOY

ASK AND YOU SHALL RECEIVE

$15 (Amazon $20)
ISBN: 978-0-9988484-8-8

The Power of Positive Words
– the Law of Attraction
– God
= Your Light and Easy Life!

This is "the secret beyond the secret"! This book will help encourage you to create and define a direction and plan for your life. I wish to share my Nine Step Method to empower everyone to feel the freedom of a light and easy life. Open your heart and your mind and journey with me to a new and more powerful, focused and loved, aware and connected You.

ASK AND YOU SHALL RECEIVE MEDITATION

Enjoy this 20-minute *Ask And You Shall Receive Meditation* in all positive words—listen to the truth about yourself and receive inspiration.

$5
UPC: 098867225629

DAILY ASKING JOURNAL

Live by Design!

To make your life light and easy, let us put the Nine Step Method into daily action by using the *Daily Asking Journal*. This Journal will help connect you with the Power of the Universe and enable you to collect and compile all your asking intentions in one place. This personal journal for your focused thoughts and positive words supports you to raise your awareness, while having an organized platform to consciously create and record your positive, happy, light, and easy life. Script your life, keep on asking God, and be a new wineskin.

$10 (Amazon $12)
ISBN: 978-0-9988484-0-2

INSPIRATION NOTEBOOK

Live inspired!

The *Inspiration Notebook* is designed as a platform to create and record your inspirations and highlights, ideas and insights, goals and plans. Daily writing enables you to experience a purposeful life with clarity. Your ongoing plans of action and written insights guide you toward your goals and direct all focus on your target. Let this personal journal hold your ideas and goals.

The *Inspiration Notebook* is a tool to help you measure your continual growth and accomplishments. Pick up a pen, and script your life in your own hand.

$10 (Amazon $12)
ISBN: 978-0-9988484-5-7

FOCUS WHEEL WORKBOOK

The *Focus Wheel Workbook* presents you with an easy exercise to engage your belief system, stay in a positive mindset, and pray into the solution. Receive Joy collected over 50 statements to help you think about excellent and praiseworthy things. Encourage yourself to increase your belief in all areas of life by expressing clarity and solid evidence in writing. This workbook also aids in believing in and focusing on your goals. Seek God first, focus on your greatness, and live by design.

$15 (Amazon $20)
ISBN: 978-0-9988484-9-5

RECEIVE INSPIRATION

Receive Inspiration contains a mix of inspirations to open the mind to receive happiness, love, prosperity, well-being, growth, focus, and allowing. Receive Joy created this encouraging CD using only positive words that we may consciously choose to remember our greatness. Let us cheer ourselves on! Be inspired!

CD, $10
UPC: 098867227227

RECEIVE BEAUTIFUL WORDS

Every word is a creation. We can choose to create love, joy, gratitude, hope, compassion, mercy, praise, and much more positivity with our words. Let us be conscious of which word we send out to achieve what we desire. Play *Receive Beautiful Words* to imprint ourselves and our environment with positive blessings. Listen and Receive Joy!

CD, $10
UPC: 098867227128

All products are available directly from Receive Joy.

To learn more visit **www.receivejoy.com**

Subscribe to our newsletter to continue your receiving of positive awareness. Please share your email address with us: **ask@receivejoy.com**

Call or text to US cell phone number
(239) 450-1240

Like and follow Receive Joy on Facebook:
www.facebook.com/ReceiveJoy

Follow Receive Joy on Instagram:
www.instagram.com/receivejoy

We are happy to hear from you and receive your positive feedback, inspiration, and miracle stories!

With Love and Gratitude,

Receive Joy   *Receive Joy*

www.ingramcontent.com/pod-product-compliance
Lightning Source LLC
Chambersburg PA
CBHW051041160426
43193CB00010B/1029